simple days

A Journal on What Really Matters

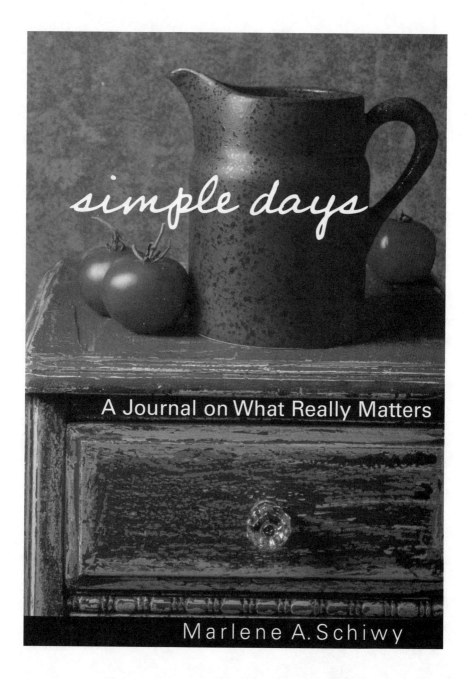

simple days

A Journal on What Really Matters

Marlene A. Schiwy

SORIN BOOKS   NOTRE DAME, INDIANA

Excerpt from "A Ritual to Read to Each Other" copyright 1960, 1998 by the Estate of William Stafford. Reprinted from *The Way It Is: New and Selected Poems* with the permission of Graywolf Press, Saint Paul, Minnesota.

Excerpt from "The Summer Day" in *House of Light* by Mary Oliver, copyright © 1990 by Mary Oliver. Reprinted by permission of Beacon Press, Boston, Massachusetts.

www.sorinbooks.com

International Standard Book Number: 1-893732-30-4

Cover design by Maurine R. Twait

Cover photograph © 2001 Garry Gay/Image Bank

Text design by Brian C. Conley

Printed and bound in the United States of America.

Library of Congress Cataloging-in-Publication Data
    Schiwy, Marlene A.
Simple days : a journal on what really matters / Marlene A. Schiwy.
    p. cm.
Includes bibliographical references.
ISBN 1-893732-30-4 (pbk.)
    1. Simplicity. 2. Schiwy, Marlene A.--Diaries. I. Title.
    BJ1496 .S36 2002
    179'.9--dc21
                                                                    CIP
                                                        2001004617

To my parents,
Lilli and Henry Schiwy,
whose quiet generosity
and joy in sharing what we had
made my childhood rich

Contents

Acknowledgments

I want to offer my heartfelt thanks to the many friends and students whose lively interest and questions about this "journal of simple living" helped keep me on track: Mary Brady, Nellie Brandt, Margery Cornwell, Jarda Crane, Marketa Goetz-Stankiewicz, Betty Jampel, Nancy Linde, Pamela Mailman, Dorald Patsos, Barbara Peretz Perlman, Elizabeth Schneider, Lisa Shumicky, Louise Tamarkin, Anne-marie Thorne, Gloria Vistica, Anne Wallace, and so many others in New York and Vancouver.

I am grateful to my agent, Rita Rosenkrantz, for her steady belief in the value of a quiet meditation on simplicity. Her integrity, courtesy, and professionalism have made her a joy to work with.

I appreciate the welcome extended to me by Julie Hahnenberg and Robert Hamma, my editors at Sorin Books. Their editorial suggestions were helpful and I want to thank them for the time and effort they generously contributed.

As always, my deepest thanks go to Steve, cherished soulmate and life companion, for his unfailing support, his sensitive and perceptive feedback, and for being bedrock.

Prologue

This is not a book about "going back to the land." It's not a book about going back to anything. We can't go back, even if we want to. We can only start from where we are today. You won't find instructions on homesteading, growing organic tomatoes, or keeping bees in these pages. Nor do I describe a desperate leap from an urban nightmare into a rural paradise. This journal moves back and forth between two major North American cities—New York and Vancouver—my two homes for the past decade.

This is a different kind of book on simple living. It's not a how-to manual offering eight or even eighteen steps to a simpler life. Nor does it promise a shortcut for clearing clutter or finding spiritual enlightenment. In fact, it doesn't promise any answers at all. The quest to live more simply is a highly personal one; therefore, I cannot tell you how to reinvent your life on a slower track.

What I can share with you is my own process—conducted during a year of journal writing—of trying to understand more and more deeply what is most precious to me, what is worth my time and love and energy. Reflections on my own experience from one day to the next provide the starting point for a year-long meditation on what it might mean to live simply and authentically, close to the bare bones of what matters most in our lives today. That is what this book is about.

The promise that *Simple Days* does hold out to you is that living simply does not have to mean moving out to the boondocks to follow Thoreau. Neither does it require you to strip your possessions down to what you can stuff into a suitcase or the trunk of your car, although there are those who prefer to live this way.

Simple living is not *simplistic* living. We don't have to play at being primitive, or shut down our highly evolved rational left brains and pretend complexity and fragmentation don't exist in the world, or deny that we may even occasionally find them exciting. We don't have to give our favorite clothes away and live forever after in a homespun sari like Gandhi and Mother Teresa, or in a pair of ratty jeans and a faded sweatshirt. Unless we want to.

The beauty of the search for simplicity is that we start where we are *right now*. Since I began writing this journal I have discovered time and time again that simple living—like journal writing itself—is an open-ended journey. There is no map that tells us how to get from here to there. We create our own path as we go.

Only you can define what living more simply means in your unique life circumstances. For one person, it might mean reevaluating a frantic involvement in too many worthy causes in order to create time for reflection and taking stock. For another, it may mean tuning into the "felt sense" of your life and getting in touch with the sources of fragmentation and conflict that drain you of energy and joy. For someone else, it might involve paying off credit card debt and getting your financial house in order. Yet another person might decide to change careers or sell the family business in order to spend more time with growing children or join the Peace Corps.

My point is that the quest for a simpler life begins with paying attention to the way we live our lives *today*. It starts with learning to see what is so close that it's invisible most of the time. Living simply demands that we take our habitual day-to-day routines off automatic pilot and look closely and fearlessly at where our lives are heading. And it requires that we discover—with all the pure single-mindedness of a child at play and the passionate curiosity of a traveler cast on some exotic foreign shore—where our own treasure lies. When we discover what that treasure is, many other things fall away. Seen for what they are—mere substitutes for an authentic experience of passion and purpose in life—they no longer fill a need, no longer clutter our horizons. This leaves us with time and space we have only dreamed of, time for what is essential, time for what matters most.

Over the course of the year, I found myself asking many questions. How does the desire for a simpler life affect my relationships and sense of community? What about my attitude toward material possessions and consumption, career and finances, spirituality and the environment, homemaking and leisure? How can I nourish body and soul, and find time for creative expression? Is it possible to live simply while earning a living? What is the relationship between inner and outer simplicity?

These are, of course, in the first instance, *my* questions. But perhaps you'll hear echoes of your own here as well.

You'll find many of my favorite quotations about simple living woven into these pages. And, because both children at play and travelers in foreign lands get hungry and delight in good food, I have included some of my favorite recipes for simple cooking. Short on preparation time and expense, they are long on nutrition and eating pleasure. I hope that they will nourish your body and soul along the way.

Introduction

*Simplicity is the most difficult thing to secure in this world;
it is the last limit of experience and the last effort of genius.*

—George Sand

When I was a little girl growing up in the Pacific Northwest of Canada, I thought we were rich because my parents gave so much away. One evening twenty-five years later my father casually mentioned that, according to Statistics Canada, our family of five had lived below the national poverty level through all the years of my childhood.

My father's offhand comment left me in shock. What I remember of those early years is the sweet, steady sense of abundance. There was always more than enough food for anyone who arrived at the door unexpectedly, which happened often in the tightly-knit German Baptist immigrant community to which we belonged. My grandmother, daughter of a German seamstress, sewed exquisite two-of-a-kind matching dresses for my younger sister, Nellie, and me, that made us the envy of our friends. By the time I was eight years old I had a job picking strawberries, raspberries, and string beans during the summer holidays. Opening my own bank account with my earnings made me feel grown up and important. Even better, it meant I could indulge my enormous hunger for books and piano music.

During my thirteenth summer I bought a top-model Olympia typewriter with my summer income, proud of my ability to purchase equipment essential to the writer I intended to become. At sixteen I went on a four-week, eight country musical tour of Europe with the local junior high school choir and band. I'd earned the money for the trip myself, washing dishes the summer before in the Empress, Chilliwack's only luxury hotel.

The very idea that the government could have classified us as poor would have struck me as absurd.

How could we be poor, when the pantry in the brand new house my father had built for us was stocked to the ceiling with every variety of homemade preserve and pickle, in all the rich glowing colors of summer; when the freezer, always filled to maximum capacity, held the side of beef and twenty-five soup chickens we purchased every year from the Schulzes, along with a steady stream of my mother's dark, moist homemade bread, the staple of my childhood diet?

How could we be poor, when the closets and drawers were filled with clothes, linens, and kitchenware my parents had bought on sale and stockpiled for future use? When we owned two vehicles, a silvery green Buick and a dark blue panel truck with "Henry Schiwy Construction" in large white letters on the side? When my parents often filled two grocery carts during our regular Friday night shopping trip, loading up the second for a family in need?

How could we be poor, when we could afford to give so much away?

True, we did not eat in restaurants, buy the latest fashions, or take expensive holidays. But neither did anyone else we knew. We recycled easily and naturally. Leftovers from one meal were incorporated into the next, often tastier than the first. Old clothes were given a second life span: adapted for a smaller size, or used in a patchwork quilt. When my father's workshirts were too far gone, they were converted into cleaning rags, the worn, soft flannel far more effective than any Jay-cloth. Accustomed to going hungry during their childhood years in wartime rural Germany, my parents did not take kindly to waste of any kind. If our family could not use something, there was always another that could.

True, the balance in my parents' bank account was never what they would have liked. There were years when my father wasn't sure from where the next mortgage payment would come. And whether it was furniture we needed or a new car, my parents waited until they could pay cash. Rarely, if ever, did we pay full price for anything. We waited until it went on sale, then bought two. Or four. Or a case.

Yet what has stayed with me over the years is that comforting assurance of plenty, with enough to spare. Hardly the memory of someone who'd experienced poverty, regardless of what Statistics Canada had decreed.

Somehow, I managed to live through my university years—more than a dozen in total—with that same sense of abundance, even when I must have known there was often barely enough money in my bank account to cover the next month's rent. Young and healthy, filled with energy and optimism, I was thrilled to be at university, only the third member of my extended family to be in that position and the first, as it turned out, to earn a Ph.D. Fortunately for me, it was respectable, almost fashionable, to be a poverty-stricken student during the 1970s, and I was no worse off than anyone else I knew.

Student loans and a variety of scholarships and part-time jobs provided a living of sorts. Rent in Vancouver was affordable then; my sister and I shared a large apartment two blocks from the ocean. Our parents continued to supply us with homemade bread and canned fruits and vegetables from their garden. I created my own and my sister's wardrobes with sewing skills patiently passed on by Oma Schiwy. Campus life at the University of British Columbia and membership in the Vancouver Bach Choir provided social interaction and a musical community. Most of what I really wanted, I managed, somehow, to have.

Then, as many of my friends were rising rapidly in their respective professional fields, I went to Europe and the Middle East, writing in my journal as I traveled, and searching for the meaning of life during the late 1970s when this was still, marginally, a respectable pastime. After six months on the road I flew home from Israel with less than fifty dollars in my pocket. When it became clear that my B.A. in English literature was not going to lead me to a rewarding job, I simply went back to university. Not to acquire a marketable degree, however, but because long days of reading and writing punctuated by stimulating two-hour cappuccino breaks with other hungry minds seemed, even on a shoestring budget, a far more appealing prospect than working at a boring dead-end job, where I'd be trading my nine-to-five for an income only slightly larger than my graduate fellowship would provide.

In 1983 I went to England on a British Commonwealth Doctoral Fellowship. The rent for my shabby but spacious room at William

Goodenough House for Postgraduate Overseas Students in Bloomsbury took more than half of my modest monthly stipend, leaving me with £35, then approximately $50, for my weekly living expenses, including food, clothing, and subway fares. Even as I subsisted on pasta and chickpeas, however, the reality of barely making it to the end of the month, once again, did not cast too great a shadow. Life seemed very good.

Willy G., as the residence was affectionately referred to, housed scholars and artists from all over the world, ensuring a ready-made social life for those who desired it. With my student ID, I could get into any concert on the South Bank for a few pounds. I was even lucky enough to find a first-rate singing teacher only too happy to exchange voice lessons for reliable childcare.

Despite being poorer than I had ever been before, or have ever been since, there was a great freedom in living, at thirty, without a mortgage, or car, or any of the other time-consuming accoutrements of adult life. My sole purpose and responsibility were to complete my doctoral dissertation on Christa Wolf, an East German writer whose work I loved. I knew even then it was a charmed life I led, filled with literature and music, friendship and community, and during my final year, love—when I met Steve, now my husband, during his sabbatical at Cambridge University.

Looking back now, it's clear that by the time I'd made it into my thirties with a richly satisfying lifestyle on a marginal income, I knew beyond question that money is not a good barometer of abundance, that there is no meaningful relationship between quality of life and material consumption—a valuable thing to have known during the infamous "decade of greed."

In 1988, having obtained my doctorate in German literature at the University of London with little thought of what I would do next, I joined Steve in New York—with no work visa, no job prospects, no source of income, and no friends. And the exhilarating communal world of graduate student life came to an abrupt end.

After a year of deep despondency over my non-status in the academic world, and riding the rollercoaster of a new full-time relationship, eventually I found several part-time teaching jobs, though scandalously ill-paid and exploitative. And I began to consider, at thirty-five, what to do with the rest of my life.

Common sense seemed to suggest that, somewhere along the way, I'd get myself a full-time job like other adults, with a proper salary and benefits. It seemed pretty unlikely that this would turn out to be an academic position in New York, since there were hundreds of applicants for every job I sought that first year. But whatever it would turn out to be, I reasoned, once I got that job and established my professional identity, I would be thrust into the real world of student loan payments and mortgages. Meanwhile I was content to teach part-time, conduct journal writing workshops for women, and write. Along the way, my first book, *A Voice of Her Own: Women and the Journal Writing Journey,* was published, and the dream that had prompted my thirteen-year-old self to purchase that Olympia typewriter was realized at last.

Then, within a year, two well-paid, full-time positions became available. The first was a tenure-track teaching post at what turned out to be the best-paid junior college in the country. Nine hundred people applied for a handful of jobs. Twenty were interviewed, myself among them. I did not receive an offer. By all rights, I should have been bitterly disappointed yet, oddly enough, I wasn't. The truth is, I'd never quite convinced myself that I really wanted the position. I would have preferred to receive an offer, to be sure. I might even have accepted it out of delighted gratitude. But deep down, I wasn't so sure that teaching four or five classes of freshman composition each semester was my calling in life. Did I really want a full-time teaching job at a busy junior college, along with endless committee work and the exhausting commute that either Steve or I would be forced to make? Not required after all to make that decision, I settled back contentedly into my poorly paid but satisfying hodgepodge of part-time careers.

The first baby boomers turned fifty in 1996. This was also the year during which, at forty-two, I began seriously to consider the financial exigencies of my future, something that would have bored me to tears in my twenties and thirties. Halfway through my adult working years, it was high time to think about making provisions for the anticipated fifteen to twenty post-retirement years that statistics say I, a healthy North American female with an average life expectancy, should plan for.

As the reality of money began to grow vivid, it suddenly seemed imperative to gain clarity about my financial philosophy and future. This coincided with a long delayed settlement involving the sale of the house from Steve's first marriage, and we had also begun to make plans for relocating to Vancouver at the turn of the century, following Steve's early retirement. Suddenly we were in the midst of number-crunching such as I had never experienced before.

As I immersed myself in pension projections and dollar amounts, I realized with surprise that I was enjoying it. Making plans for our early (if modest) financial independence was exhilarating. I also began to think about the literal and symbolic significance of money—something we don't really do in this culture—and to glimpse how deeply our attitudes about its importance in our every-day lives affect every other dimension of our lives. Jungian analyst Helen Luke's brilliant essay, "Money and the Feminine Principle of Relatedness," and *Your Money or Your Life* by Joe Dominguez and Vicki Robin, provided two very different, complementary perspectives of value. In the process of reading them, I found myself bringing into focus my dearest values and priorities, not least the question of how and where I wanted to invest my life energy.

Then another full-time career opportunity presented itself. I felt I had to take this one seriously since it was so lucrative. It was clear that if I took on a high-profile job with occasional weekend responsibilities, our entire quality of life would change beyond recognition. Up to an alarm at 6 a.m., I'd be out the door by the time Steve woke up. His late teaching schedule would mean that we'd hardly see each other three days of the week.

Gone would be our leisurely breakfasts of coffee and blueberry corn muffins, discussing our dreams to the insistently joyful strains of Bach's oboe music. Gone, the luxurious days of writing and reading, planning workshops and courses. Gone, too, our late afternoon walks on the boardwalk with that endless horizon of ocean stretching out before us. We would need a second car. I'd have to acquire a professional wardrobe. We'd have to eat out or bring in prepared food more often. I would no longer be able to move so freely or frequently between New York and Vancouver, between my east coast and west coast lives. My teaching, writing, and workshops would fall by the wayside as I recast my life to meet the demands of a new career. Our entire life together would have to be reinvented. In essence, as Steve put it, accepting the job would mean a 180 degree change of direction, with an abrupt end to everything I had lovingly tended for half a dozen years and was finally seeing the fruits of. Even my dreams told me I didn't want the job.

And yet. And yet.

I also knew that accepting that position would provide a sense of professional identity I'd never known, and a salary three times what I'd earned to date. And it would give me a pension, something I could no longer afford to shrug off as casually as I did a decade earlier.

I took a full week to think and feel my way through this possibility and, when we were both sure, I turned it down. But I am grateful for the chance to have recognized that, apart from my marginal income and lack of benefits, *I already was doing work that held great meaning for me*, work that seemed to flow out of my deepest and most authentic being. Why would I give up my work and our cherished, shared daily rhythm for a demanding position that in my heart of hearts I knew I didn't want, just so that five or ten years later I'd be able to quit and come back to what I'm doing now? What guarantee was there that I'd even be around to cash in on this deferred gratification, five years down the line?

During the months that followed I reasoned that, perhaps instead of earning more, I simply had to continue the habits of frugality learned during my childhood and honed over a lifetime of being a student and part-time wage earner. What if I could simply continue to live this life of freedom with my soulmate beside me, both of us content to trade income for time? If abstaining from the baby boomers' infamous love of material luxury could grant us the autonomy we crave, what more could we want?

Above all, what became crystal clear to me was just how precious my time is. More precious than money, security, and a good benefits package. More precious even than prestige or public recognition. In the end, I just couldn't imagine trading the freedom of our life together for greater financial prosperity, which is, quite simply, what it came down to.

Time. Energy. Lifeblood.

All that any of us has, in the end.

And I began to pay more attention to what I did with my time, how I "spent" it, inhabited it, and filled it with meaning. I also began to notice how the people around me "invested" theirs.

For it wasn't simply a job I was saying "yea" or "nay" to. It was a radical shift in my way of dwelling in the world. And the questions that continued to bubble beneath the surface of my calm and resolute "nay" were absolutely fundamental.

What matters most?

How much is enough?

What is my life energy for?

How will I spend my days?

What is essential and what superfluous?

And so, I did what I always do when I want to understand something down to its roots and all the way through: I turned to my journal. I began to write down my thoughts, feelings, and questions in order to observe more clearly the sense of purpose shaping my day-to-day living. And to determine how I could bring the necessities of my existence more clearly into the foreground.

"I want a singleness of eye, a purity of intention, a central core to my life," Anne Morrow Lindbergh wrote in her timeless *Gift from the Sea*. This journal is my attempt to create synthesis and harmony out of complex alternatives and to discover, more clearly, my own purity of intention. In writing it, I wanted to delve more deeply into the underlying pattern of my days and to determine what they hold. I wanted to explore what simple living might mean for me and perhaps for others asking similar questions. More than anything else, I wanted to see—in true and vivid colors—what matters most to me.

The original text of this journal was hand-written in four Clairefontaine notebooks, purple, plum, royal blue, and turquoise, approximately five hundred pages in total. I could have written it on the word processor, saving countless hours and making it a much more efficient process. But there is no real pleasure for me in front of the computer, even though I would not be without it during later stages of preparation. A lifelong diarist, I spent many rich, enjoyable hours with those notebooks instead, designating set colors of ink for particular topics, and enjoying the visible growth of this project from one volume to two, then to three, and finally wrapping it up halfway through the fourth notebook.

Although I wrote this "Journal on What Really Matters" for publication, I also ended up weaving in occasional entries from my personal journal which continued during this period. The relationship between them was fluid at times. I have condensed and edited the original journal manuscript in order to avoid unnecessary repetition and to offer the greatest possible clarity. In several instances I altered names in order to protect the privacy of others. In all other respects I have written and edited this journal with the greatest truthfulness and factual accuracy I could manage.

Simple Days:
A Journal on
What Really Matters

Be patient toward all that is unsolved in your heart and try to love the questions themselves *like locked rooms and like books that are written in a very foreign tongue. Do not now seek the answers, which cannot be given you because you would not be able to live them. And the point is, to live everything.* Live *the questions now. Perhaps you will then gradually, without noticing it, live along some distant day into the answer.*

—Rainer Maria Rilke, "Letters to a Young Poet"

October 29th

I just filled my huge new black café au lait cup with strong Colombian coffee. Albinoni is rippling joyously in the background and sunlight is touching everything in the room with gold. It's my favorite kind of morning, when everything seems possible and nothing is more precious than this freedom I have to get up at leisure and contemplate how to shape the day.

There's something wonderful—and privileged, I know—in waking up without an alarm clock and determining the day's rhythm: writing, teaching preparation, a little cleaning, a long walk, and perhaps some baking for my Wednesday night women's writing group. Most people don't have that luxury and I try not to take it for granted.

Lately I have been reading several books on the theme of simple living. I begin with great interest, but then, all too soon, disappointment sets in. Too many detailed instructions for beekeeping, organic farming, and duck raising. Reading, I feel impatient. This may all be informative, but it doesn't address the questions that fascinate me.

What matters most?

How much is enough?

What prompts people to simplify their lives?

And I don't mean just to talk about it. Almost everyone I know wants to simplify, cut back, and unclutter, but only a few actually are able to do it. Who manages to simplify, and how? What makes them different from the others?

For that matter, what does "simple living" mean? What is it we yearn for when we talk about wanting a simpler life? How can we even hope to live simply in such a crazy and chaotic world? And what alternatives are there to leaving the city in order to raise chickens and sheep, which doesn't appeal to me in the least? How significant a role does money play in this quest? Bringing these questions closer to home, what does simple living mean to *me*? My life, compared to many, is relatively simple already, so why does this theme continue to intrigue me?

These are some of the questions I want to explore in this journal. I don't know if I'll find answers, but since the questions have been reverberating in my mind for several years now, perhaps it's time to bring them to the light of conscious attention. In any case, Rilke promised his young poet that if he "lived the questions" with all his heart, he might eventually begin to live the answers. That sounds good to me.

October 30th

This morning I steamed and puréed butternut squash for pumpkin bread. I don't know why I feel such a powerful urge to "put food up" for the winter, but since I seem compelled to do it, I'll indulge myself today. This is my favorite recipe for pumpkin bread.

Pumpkin Walnut Bread (two loaves)

2 cups whole wheat flour
1 cup unbleached all-purpose flour
1/3 cup oats, or wheat germ, or wheat bran, or oat bran
2 tsp. baking soda
1 tsp. baking powder
1 T. cinnamon
1 tsp. nutmeg (optional)
1/2 tsp. salt
1/2 cup canola oil or melted butter
1 1/3 cups sugar (adjust amount as desired)
1 tsp. vanilla
4 eggs
2 cups cooked pumpkin or any winter squash (e.g., acorn
    or butternut)

2/3 cup water (or milk or soymilk)
3/4 cup raisins
3/4 cup chopped walnuts or pecans

Sift together all dry ingredients except sugar in a bowl. Beat together oil, sugar, and vanilla in a large bowl. Add eggs, one by one, beating well after each. Stir in pumpkin and water. Add flour mixture, stirring just until smooth. Stir in raisins and walnuts. Bake in two loaf pans, at 350° F for 50-60 minutes. Let loaves cool in the pan for 20 minutes, then put on rack or plate. This is a tasty, low-fat, and nutritious autumn breakfast loaf. I make it often, sometimes doubling this recipe. It freezes well.

Later . . .

As the spicy aroma of pumpkin bread floats into the living room, I realize that one of my guiding principles has always been: Never make one of anything. I've inherited this from my mother, I'm sure. Mum always thinks big, even now with only two of them at home. Twenty loaves of bread, four dozen cabbage rolls, five or six apple cakes. You never know when company might come, or who might appreciate receiving a gift of food. So, if I'm going to measure out the ingredients for a pumpkin loaf, I might as well make two, or better still, four. One to enjoy now, one for a friend, and two for the freezer. When I buy chicken and vegetables for soup, I often make two large pots at once: one with pasta, for Steve; another with potatoes, for me.

I used to think that I was the only one daft enough to make enormous pots of soup for a household of two, but Laurence does it too. Even though she lives alone, she cooks up huge batches of spaghetti sauce, often several kinds at once. When I visited her in Montreal this spring, she had just put ten liters of meat sauce into the freezer. When she makes borscht, she does the same. That way she can decide in the morning what she wants to eat for dinner, and always has a variety of tasty, nutritious, and trouble-free meals to choose from.

Cooking large quantities of food at once makes me feel that my time is wisely used, that I'm taking good care of Steve and myself. Like my mother and Laurence, I get pleasure from the look of the counter covered with delicious food, the little freezer filled with things I have made, and the feeling that our bodily needs are well provided for. The same thing is true when I sew. I rarely make one of anything. I make many quilts, several skirts from the same pattern, multiple versions of whatever it is. As if I want to clothe the whole family.

Abundance. It's always such a theme and such a value for me.

October 31st

What *is* most important to me at this time in my life?

Time. More than anything else, I value having control over my own life energy.

Independence. Being able to come and go as I like, to alter my routine as I feel inclined, and to work when and where I choose: at home, on the plane, in New York, in Vancouver. I'd like to get to the point where I don't depend on the quiet of my study but can write wherever I find myself.

Integrity. In our age of endless fragmentation, I need to experience my life as whole, woven of a single cloth. I know what my most cherished priorities are, and I do my best to live accordingly.

Creative expression. When inspiration strikes, I can turn to my journal, plan a workshop, write a song, bake a Black Forest cherry cake, sew a robe or a gypsy skirt.

Friendship. Having intimate relationships in which I genuinely see and am seen by the other person.

Community. I have found this difficult in New York, much easier in Vancouver, with my long-standing circle of friends there, and in London, with new university friends and colleagues and the people at William Goodenough Residence. New York is a tough nut. Here my community is the one I have created over the years with my Women's Journal Workshop.

November 1st

What exactly does simplicity mean? Getting rid of outdated clutter? Spending less time on activities that aren't necessary or meaningful? Savoring every day of our lives more fully? Getting more deeply in touch with our own inner process? Doing more with less? Cultivating patience, kindness, and compassion toward all life? Being less neurotic in our emotional lives, more direct about our needs? All of these?

Even during the years of Nazi terror in Europe, Etty Hillesum, the young Dutch Jewish writer, was so clear about the importance of simplicity in her life. On the first of April, 1942, she confided to her journal her fervent wish:

> To be very unobtrusive, and very insignificant, always striving for more simplicity. Yes, to become simple and live simply, not only within yourself but also in your everyday dealings. Don't make ripples all around you, don't try so hard to be interesting, keep your distance, be honest, fight the desire to be thought fascinating by the outside world. Instead, reach for true simplicity in your inner life and in your surroundings, and also work.[1]

When we "reach for true simplicity," what is it we are reaching for?

November 4th

It really is, as Mum has always said, possible to live very simply as far as material things are concerned. But my version of the good life isn't that of Scott and Helen Nearing, those early advocates of voluntary simplicity and leaders of the "back to the earth" movement. In one of her books, Helen explains,

> Living the good life for us was practicing harmony with the earth and all that lives on it. It was earning enough by the sweat of our brows, beholden to no employer or job. It was growing our own food, building our own buildings, cutting our own wood, and providing for our own livelihood. We needed and used little money. If we couldn't pay for a thing, we made it ourselves or did without. Our idea was to take care of our physical needs, housing, food, fuel, and clothing so that we could read, write, study, teach, or make music without dependence on the outside world, and to do this together.[2]

I can't honestly see Steve and myself doing large-scale organic gardening and living off the harvest all year. We don't even like getting our hands dirty! What the Nearings referred to as "bread labor" would have to mean something different for us. For me, right now, it involves earning enough money through part-time teaching to pay the bills and save as much as possible, so that in several years we can buy a house with a minimal mortgage or none at all. Once that is taken care of, I too would like to be as self-sufficient as possible. Again, this will mean something different for Steve and me than it did for the Nearings, since we are more likely to be living in Vancouver than in the country. But, like them, I'll continue to make things myself whenever I can and enjoy the fact that what I create is both of better quality and less expensive than its ready-made equivalent.

I imagine my daily rhythm will look a little different from theirs, as well. Up at 7 or 8 a.m. for coffee and muffins, I'll write until mid-afternoon, then go out for a run or long walk before dinner. In the evenings, I'll teach a weekly writing workshop or two, perhaps a college writing class. Then some "arts and crafts," a weekly choir rehearsal, and once or twice a week, dinner and a walk with a friend. In some respects, come to think of it, my life isn't all that different from this, even now. No nine-to-five job for me, if I can avoid it. I like owning my own time.

November 6th

Our societal obsession with material possessions continues to fascinate me. There are so many things we *don't* need at the local mall. Now that I'm paying attention, I realize how much of my shopping in the past has been recreational. Although I've never been a big spender, over the years I have bought plenty of clothes, cosmetics, and other items on impulse, only to regret it afterward. If I had the money for all the clothes I've bought two sizes too small as inspiration to lose weight, I could purchase a whole new wardrobe!

Steve and I are at midlife. We probably have enough durable material things to last us the rest of our lives, if necessary. If I consider that every item I might buy represents a certain expenditure of my life energy, there's very little I *must* have. I own my life, and enjoy a great freedom that most people only dream of.

Many people don't even realize they have a choice about the way they live. Too often we believe that we *need* everything we *want*, and fail to see the difference. Only rarely do we derive all the use we can from the things we already have. We replace them—clothes, appliances, furniture, cars—for novelty, for more up-to-date, exciting, attractive versions. And acquiring new things does provide a certain rush of adrenaline; I know about that. But then what? More "stuff" to organize and keep track of, to store and eventually recycle or throw out.

How can we resist that cycle of buying and consuming what we don't need? More important, what inner needs are we trying to fill by acquiring more and more unnecessary material goods? It reminds me of when I visited Alexandra in Bonn in the summer of 1985 and saw bathroom shelves stuffed with more cosmetics than anyone could use in the course of two lifetimes. Every cupboard, nook and cranny of her bathroom was crammed. Knowing that she felt lonely and cut off from her family in Athens, I wondered how much of her shopping was compensatory, an attempt to ease the emotional isolation she experienced living on her own in Germany.

What about my own "stuff"? I'm hoping to clear out about a third of our material clutter. Especially clothes. Anything I haven't worn in a long time goes to Project Hospitality for the homeless. The closets are bursting and I don't even wear most of these clothes. My entire study needs drastic streamlining too. By the time we're ready to move, I want to have a clear idea of just how many of our possessions we really need to ship across the continent.

"Simplicity, simplicity, simplicity," Thoreau reminded himself, just to make sure he got the point. Always the best advice I can give myself, as well.

November 11th

I am grading *Mrs. Dalloway* essays and wondering once again who plagiarized and who didn't. I'm tired of reading woefully inadequate papers, and I'm not even convinced that I can teach my students how to write better ones, given the present combination of ill-prepared students and overcrowded classes. I do enjoy the classroom discussion, but as far as the written work goes, it's discouraging to see, over and over again, how few skills most students have in critical thinking, and how disinterested many of them are in expanding those skills. How can I teach them otherwise *and* teach them "Modern Culture" in fourteen weeks, especially with classes that are far too large?

Once we leave New York, I may just decide not to teach at the university level again. I want to work with people who are there voluntarily, who are eager to learn, who are prepared and willing to take the plunge. Rereading *Your Money or Your Life* is reminding me that I have limited life energy and that endless hours spent grading poorly written and sometimes plagiarized or bought student essays is not how I want to use it. Once we see how our finances work out in Vancouver, I shouldn't have to. As much as possible, I want to work at things I really believe in and find challenging, rewarding, and worthwhile. I want to be able to use what is best in me, and college teaching doesn't always call on that.

November 12th

I've been thinking about the relationship between simple living and journal writing. They seem to go together so naturally, I suppose because both are spiritual quests—attempts to get closer to the soul's true essence.

Journal writing supports my search for a simpler life by helping me to stay conscious. Instead of looking outward for satisfaction of my needs and for emotional rewards, the journal allows me to tap into the depths of my inner experience. It helps me make clear what is most important to me and to keep that in front of my eyes while I sift through the extraneous clutter and rubble in my life. It has become my form of meditation, of thinking and feeling on paper.

At best, I believe, our journals become an ongoing conversation with our souls that helps us become aware of the incessant chatter of the ego. It's also a way of integrating all the fragments of our lives, of bringing everything together in a meaningful mosaic. At least in this one place, then, we can see our lives as a whole. Simple living, in turn, creates the time and space for journal writing that could so easily be cluttered with a multitude of tasks and errands of all kinds. It allows us to discover the inner riches far more lasting than any material wealth.

Keeping a journal plays an important role in so many of the published accounts of people who opt for simpler lifestyles. In one of my favorites, *Simple Living: One Couple's Search for a Better Life,* Wanda Urbanska and Frank Levering describe their decision to leave their fast-paced lives in Los Angeles and relocate to the Blue Ridge Mountains of Virginia in order to take over the family orchard. They write,

> In Los Angeles we had lived fast but not well. Often short on cash, but always long on professional ambition, we'd saved little time for each other or for the day-to-day rewards of small but significant things—watching a sunset, keeping a journal. . . . We were here to simplify our lives. To find the time as well as the means to do the things that mattered most.[3]

Joe Dominguez and Vicki Robin (*Your Money or Your Life*) for their part recommend writing out detailed responses to key questions such as "What brings you the most fulfillment—and how is that related to money?" and "If you didn't have to work for a living, what would you do with your time?" They also ask:

> What about your relationship with yourself? . . . What if you had the time you needed to write in a journal . . . and contemplate the inner and outer horizons? Being able to reflect on your life while you're living it . . . is one key to fulfillment.[4]

Carol Orsborn (*Enough Is Enough*) describes registering for a journal class after she made the decision to cut back on her work hours and figure out what she really wanted to do with her time. After years of making it big in the business world, she says she became terrified of "the never-ending gray sameness that accompanied my fifty-hour work weeks, exhausted routines and relationships."[5] As she began to make the necessary changes, she discovered new joy in her marriage, children, and friendships, and time to write in her journal. Betty Jane Wylie (*Enough*), who sold her spacious apartment in Toronto and moved to an isolated lakeside cottage more than a decade ago, tells us that her favorite recommendation for simplifying is: "Keep a journal."

It's clear that people who have a yearning to unclutter their lives are on an inner journey. A profound shift in consciousness is taking place, and keeping a journal is often their way of exploring and trying to articulate what it means. Next spring I want to offer a workshop on "Journal Writing and the Art of Simple Living." It will allow me to think further about the relationship between the two, and I know the topic will generate great interest in the workshop community. So many are on their own quests to streamline and simplify.

November 13th

I went to the mall for the first time in ages last night. I wanted to get my father's dress shirts before the holiday crowds get enormous and to pick up a few things at the health food store. From the time I arrived, I couldn't wait to get out of there. All the Christmas hype was such a turnoff, and I didn't feel like looking at things with the semi-conscious hope of becoming interested enough to buy something. The only thing that caught my eye was a small black Coach handbag at Macy's, for $180. All I could think of was that, with the assortment of handbags I have already, I could not justify trading in that many hours of life energy for one more. I must have about a dozen handbags already, only three or four of which I regularly use. What a good feeling not to believe that buying something will make me feel good. I literally felt a sense of relief as I headed to the car to drive back to the College of Staten Island and grade papers while waiting for Steve to finish teaching.

November 15th

Today I want to write about gifts. Gifts both given and received. Perhaps because my parents always gave so freely wherever it was needed, I discovered early on how much joy there is in giving.

Just after my seventh birthday in 1960, my mother's Uncle Emil and his family arrived at our front door after a risky escape from East Berlin. In order to avoid suspicion, they'd traveled separately. He left with his two young sons and his wife took their teenage daughter. The Bucholtzes came with nothing but the clothes on their backs and two small suitcases. Since they couldn't carry anything that would have alerted the border authorities to their planned escape, they left with only a change of clothing for each. For years afterward I pictured their home in East Germany, full of shabby comforts, waiting patiently for its inhabitants to return.

What I remember of Christmas that year is our small, noisy house filled with the rich, spicy aroma of Pfefferkuchen and Stollen—and with people. Ten of us shared three bedrooms and a single bathroom for more than six weeks. I had hoarded my ten-cents-a-week allowance for the entire year and bought presents for fifteen people with the five dollars I'd saved: plastic napkin holders for my aunts, cotton handkerchiefs for the men, rubber balls for the children. I don't recall what I got for Christmas that year, or how my lovingly chosen baubles were received, but I do remember the pleasure of shopping with my beloved Aunt Irma in the old Woolworth's store on Wellington Avenue for these small items.

Today, gift giving is most often symbolic. We want to express love and caring in concrete and material form. But there must be better ways to celebrate the importance of our relationships than scratching our heads every year, wondering what to get someone who already has everything they need and want, suspecting all the while that we're merely adding to their clutter. A gift holds meaning, I think, when it has something of the giver in it, when it's something made with love—a quilt or a cake, for example. But if it's a matter of running into a store at the last minute, desperately hoping to spot something suitable, the meaning is lost. What's scarce these days is more often *time* than material goods. So why not let that be my gift? Time and care made tangible, in the form of freshly baked bread or some other kind of practical nurturance.

Over the years I have given and received so many gifts, but the ones that have given me the greatest pleasure are those I made, or that were made for me. Family and friends have given me knitted scarves and vests, homesewn embroidered nightgowns, pottery, exquisite framed needlework, wooden jewelry boxes and sewing baskets, mahogany bookcases and a cedar chest, handmade journals, several knitted afghans, and wicker baskets full of homemade delectables. I, in turn, have made dresses, pantsuits, blouses, skirts, robes, nightgowns and pajamas, handbags and cushions with beadwork and embroidery, and quilts. In the winter of 1982, the Christmas before I left for England, Kathie and I made more than two dozen kinds of Christmas cookies, squares, and chocolates, filling forty wicker baskets with our delicious goodies. What pleasure we had in assembling those baskets and anticipating the joy they would bring to those who would receive them.

Nellie celebrates her fortieth birthday next March. I want to make her a "nap quilt" and then stop with birthday gifts for a while. Next year for Christmas, I want to give only gifts I've made myself. If I don't manage that, perhaps gift certificates for books or music. I simply don't have space to keep accumulating trinkets, no matter how appealing, and I bet my family and friends are in the same predicament. Maybe it's time to call a stop.

November 16th

The subject of simplicity arose in my women's book group last night. Susan and Laura said they couldn't possibly simplify in any meaningful way because they're married with children. With no children of my own, I didn't want to sound arrogant, but I suspect there are areas in which they could simplify, things they haven't considered changing.

We accept many things as unquestionably necessary. But even children, it seems to me, *need* only food and a roof over their heads, education and medical coverage, and a lot of unconditional love. Everything else—extravagant toys and clothing, expensive vacations, and eight kinds of extracurricular activities—is open for discussion. Unless we hold responsibility for extended family members or face other extenuating circumstances, there surely are ways to get more of what we really want, if not everything at once—as Mary Catherine Bateson suggests in *Composing a Life,* her wonderful discussion of women's lives. Especially when what we really want is an hour a day for ourselves.

Certain things are essential to our lives. But our idea of what these are would surely change radically if we really believed that our time on earth is limited. Friendship, community, creative expression, solitude, and time to feed the soul—these have all suffered because of our blind haste to get ahead, to have more, to succeed. What a high price we have paid along the way.

November 19th

In a week or two, after the home equity loan is paid off, Steve will finally receive the bankdraft for his share of the house from his first marriage. At last the time has come and we can begin to plan our financial future. Since we are planning to buy a house when we relocate to Vancouver in three years, one aspect of living simply right now has to do with selective frugality. By this I mean being very conscious of where and how I spend money.

Perhaps the secret is always to keep one's material desires modest and low-key. Spend less than you earn, and, if you get a raise or come into some unexpected money, sock it away. Pretend it isn't there. Because the key to financial security doesn't lie as much in how much we earn, as in how much we spend. If I earn $30,000 a year and manage to save $10,000, I am obviously better off than someone who earns $60,000 and saves only $5,000. And, of course, I'm far ahead of someone who runs up debts living beyond their means, regardless of what their salary is. For me, for us, the key to financial independence ("FI," as Joe Dominguez and Vicki Robin refer to it in *Your Money or Your Life*) will be how much we can manage to save in the next three or four years. If we can avoid a mortgage, we'll enjoy tremendous freedom.

I hope Steve and I never go into debt. We'll either pay cash or wait until we can afford to buy outright. I'm simply not willing to spend precious hours working to pay off interest on credit cards or bank loans. Right now, we share one credit card and pay the balance in full each month. That's how we want to keep it.

November 21st

What I value so much about the freedom I enjoy from one day to the next is that I can get up when I want most mornings and ask myself, what do I want to do today? When I'm writing, I go to my study for three or four hours at a time. When I'm grading essays, I spread out at the dining room table, put a load of laundry in the washer or a pot of soup on the stove, and work away at various tasks at once. The house is quiet, or I play music that suits my mood. I put the kettle on, make my coffee, and I work. I get up to stir the soup, then pick up where I left off. I don't have to fight crowds or pollution or noise on buses, ferries, or subways. The College is a twelve-minute drive away. Almost anything I really need is within walking distance. If only our immediate environment were more pleasing to the eye, if the horrendous litter and angry drivers on Richmond Road didn't put such a damper on my enjoyment of our local walks.

More so than most people with whom I've spoken, my life feels whole to me. There's no major shifting among my roles as professor, workshop leader, writer, and friend. Each brings to the fore a different dimension of my personality and temperament, but they share an underlying commonality.

Anne Morrow Lindbergh wrote, during her island retreat, in *Gift from the Sea:*

> What a wonderful day, I think, turning it around in my hand to its starting point again. What has made it so perfect? Is there not some clue here in the pattern of this day? To begin with, it is a pattern of freedom. Its setting has not been cramped in space or time. . . . Nor has the day been limited in kinds of activity. It has a natural balance of physical, intellectual and social life. It has an easy unforced rhythm. Work is not deformed by pressure.[6]

I am fortunate enough to be able to live by that "pattern of freedom" she described: the various kinds of creative work and the "natural balance of physical, intellectual, and social life." For as long as I can remember, I have craved a satisfying blend of these elements. Must be my Libra nature again, always searching for the perfect balance. I wonder if Anne was also born under the sign of the scales.

November 23rd

I've been thinking about the paradox involved in writing a journal with the intention of publishing it. Since the journal is such a private form, why not write a nonfiction book organized around specific topics instead? I suppose the challenge and fascination of this format are that it reveals the process over time, not just the distilled wisdom I hope to have gleaned at the end of the year. It's an incremental form where each entry builds on what has been written before, even while it returns, spiral-like, to familiar themes and issues. This is what has always fascinated me about the journal; no beginning or end, just the rich accretion of many major and minor insights, and the gradual emergence of significant threads and motifs. That's what prompted me to write my book on women's journals.

But I'm sure that anyone who writes a journal with publication in mind struggles with what to put in and what to leave out. Although this is not my personal journal, it does touch on private dimensions of my life. And yet—and this, I suppose, is the reason I hope it will be of interest to others—I don't think it is *only* personal. The specifics of my own experience provide the opportunity to ask questions that are important to many people.

In *The House by the Sea,* one of her published journals, May Sarton wrote, "If there is an art to the keeping of a journal intended for publication yet at the same time a very personal record, it may be in what E. Bowen said: 'One must regard oneself impersonally as an instrument.'"[7] Perhaps I am writing this journal both as someone who is representative of "the modern condition" and as someone who has made enough offbeat choices so as to have a little distance and a different perspective. In some respects I have always felt like an outsider, in part because I just didn't share the commonly accepted definition of the good life.

November 25th

Today I gave myself a gift. I took a mental health day and canceled my evening class. My students, I'm sure, laden with end-of-term assignments, also saw it as a gift. I walked, baked Pfefferkuchen, and washed the kitchen floor, then brewed a pot of espresso and settled in for a long chat with Mum. The stolen hours were delicious.

I have been thinking about some of the things I am doing right now on a practical level to make my life as stress- and clutter-free as possible. I value my time more than anything else and try not to do things from a questionable sense of obligation or merely for strategic ends. For the past two years, I've more or less lived in pants, making wardrobe maintenance efficient and easy. Four pairs of casual pants and leggings, two pairs of dress pants, and two dozen shirts and T-shirts constitute my day-to-day wardrobe. I wear hardly any makeup, saving time and money spent applying and removing it. We do less housework than I ever could have imagined and survive quite well in a more or less clean house (last Valentine's Day I drew a large heart with our initials in the dust on the piano bench). I belong to very few groups and organizations. All bills are paid by return post, so I never have to worry about forgetting or losing them. Occasionally I give myself days off to putter around and always end up surprised at how much I accomplish. I don't go shopping. I try to communicate as clearly as I can with others and have stopped feeling inadequate in situations where small talk is required. Since work and leisure are largely the same, I move freely among various activities whenever I need a change.

It's a good start, I think, but there's a long way to go.

November 26th

Last night I made Pfefferkuchen, my annual token gesture of Christmas baking. Its rich and nutty aroma is the scent of Christmas for me, not surprisingly, since the two houses in which I grew up were always filled with the scent of cinnamon, chocolate, nutmeg, cloves, and anise during the weeks before the holidays.

Christmas never did quite live up to its promise, but the promise itself never dies, it seems. Every year I still expect something extraordinary, even while I know I'll never again experience the enchantment I felt thirty years ago as Nellie and I lay on Charlotte Eichstadt's living room floor by candlelight and heard Bach's "Christmas Oratorio" from beginning to end while nibbling on bittersweet chocolate-covered Lebkuchen. Nor will I ever recapture the delicious anticipation of returning from our church's Christmas Eve program with our paper bags filled with goodies, and waiting for Oma and Opa Schiwy to arrive so we could begin unwrapping the presents under the tree.

Christmas was always the high point in our lives, the long-anticipated glowing emerald and ruby jewel of the year. In part, because it lasted so long. In late November, the anticipation would begin to mount as Mum baked Stollen, Pfeffernüsse, Pfefferkuchen, and Spritzgebäck. She'd fill enormous, thirty-pound white plastic honey pails with her Christmas baking and hide them in the cellar, warning us to stay away. We didn't, of course. We dipped in at every opportunity, hoping she wouldn't notice as the cookie level sank, inch by inch.

Around the same time I made my Christmas shopping list. In my diary, I'd note my ideas about who would get what that year. I adored the whole process of planning and shopping, wrapping and tagging gifts, rich with the anticipation of shared pleasure on Christmas Eve.

As Christmas drew nearer we'd plunge into an unprecedented flurry of social activity, mostly church- and school-related. Extra choir rehearsals for various Christmas programs, and drama practice for the Sunday School's Christmas pageant where, year after year, I was a plump, dark-haired Mary in the nativity scene, and not the beautiful angel of the Lord I so longed to be. Year after year, golden-haired, blue-eyed Rosie Schultz got to be the angel.

On Christmas Eve the tall tree was gloriously lit and our shabby little church shimmered with magic. All of the children couldn't wait for the program to end and to collect the traditional Christmas bag full of candy, nuts, mandarin oranges, and a large Jersey Milk chocolate bar. Sometimes our Sunday School teachers would give us books as well, always with a religious theme, of course.

Then home to our own Christmas tree and the presents beckoning beneath it. After all the gifts had been duly opened and admired—at first helter-skelter and as we grew older, at a more leisurely pace—we'd sit around and eat Mum's Christmas goodies, chocolate marzipan, and mandarin oranges, until late. The fireplace cast an hypnotic glow and we'd gaze into the flames until our eyes wouldn't stay open any longer, then reluctantly head off to bed.

Whatever the tensions and animosities at play in our home (and they were fierce at times), I think we did then, at least for a time, feel like a family. There was a sense of belonging to the larger community as well, and of emotional safety, as we were warmly enclosed in our cozy, festive house, everyone on their best behavior and a nasty outbreak unlikely. At least this is how my memory resurrects it these many years later.

Pfefferkuchen

3 1/2 cups unbleached flour (I use up to half whole wheat)
2 T. cocoa
4–5 tsp. baking powder
1 1/2 cups sugar
1/2 tsp. cinnamon
1/2 tsp. cloves
1/2 tsp. lemon extract or 1 tsp. lemon rind
1 cup honey or syrup
2 eggs
5 T. milk
1/2 cup softened butter (1 stick)
1 cup hazelnuts, lightly toasted and ground

Sift together flour, cocoa, and baking powder.

Mix together sugar, spices, lemon, honey, eggs, and milk.

Pour liquid mixture into middle of dry ingredients and knead until thoroughly blended.

Add butter and nuts quickly so the dough does not become sticky.

Put in refrigerator for an hour (or for up to 3 days).

Roll out dough on a floured surface and cut out with cookie cutters, OR pat with your hands into a low cake pan so dough is 3/4 inch thick.

Bake cookies 10–15 minutes; cake 15–20 minutes, at 375 degrees.

When cool, you can decorate them with your favorite icing, or simply melt chocolate chips and coat cake or cookies with chocolate. Cut cake into 2 inch squares.

November 27th

These days I feel I'm merely writing on the surface when I make an entry in here. It feels deeper than that to me in my bones, but when I sit down to write, what comes out is a little bit of this and that. And the essence of simplicity, if there is such a thing, seems to elude me here in the journal, as it does, so often, in life itself.

I am wondering how the way I channel my energy is related to simplicity. Perhaps the time and effort we devote to anything—cleaning the house, running errands, or entertaining guests—should be directly related to how joyfully we can do the task. Maybe the point is to do as many things as possible because one believes in their intrinsic value—because they are meaningful, enjoyable, and add to the quality of life, and, at the same time, minimize time spent on tasks that are irksome, unrewarding, and don't hold authentic significance for us. There is nothing inherently admirable about having a clean house, for example, but there will be a degree of cleanliness that satisfies my need for order without draining energy from my other pursuits. It will be "just clean enough"—and won't violate my desire for simplicity.

I would willingly spend time with a friend in need, or make things myself that I could buy if the quality is better, or write at length in my journal, no matter how busy I am. I will always make time for a long afternoon walk with Steve or a telephone chat with a workshop member or with a student who needs to talk. These are all things that hold unquestionable value for me. And I have kept my vow to fly home to British Columbia twice a year throughout my years of living in New York, no matter how costly. In part, because I love to be there, but above all, because I know how much it means to my parents, especially my mother. It was always clear to me that this was one of my top priorities.

On the other hand, among the things I don't devote much time or energy to are cleaning, ironing and taking clothes to the dry cleaner, sending Christmas cards, trying to keep our rental home in good repair while the landlord does nothing, grading students' reading quizzes, doing publicity for the workshop, maintaining my wardrobe, makeup, and hair, cooking elaborate meals, networking for strategic ends, or joining organizations. Clearly I must feel that these activities are not priorities.

But, how do the practical and spiritual dimensions of simple living relate to each other? Our search for simplicity can't just be for personal gain, as Steve says. It must also relate to the world around us. Caught up in legal suits, divorce settlements, IRS hassles, and too many other forms of bureaucratic madness, how do we remain peaceful and compassionate? How can we rise above things we are inexorably dragged into against our will? There is a lot of that around, and it's not so easy to avoid. Getting rid of the car would be one way to cut down on red tape, but this isn't feasible for us while we're living on Staten Island and traveling to the College three or four times a week. It would create a whole new set of complications, since public transportation leaves much to be desired here. One day, perhaps. . . .

November 28th

American Thanksgiving today. Canadian Thanksgiving coincides with Columbus Day in the United States, so I'm officially thankful twice each autumn. Above all, for Steve. And for our warm apartment and our good health and spirits, for my friends in New York, for the tremendous freedom we enjoy, and for our prospects of moving back to the mountains in three or four years. And not least, for the turkey in the oven.

I'm thankful, at forty-three, to have my grandfather, who celebrates his hundredth birthday in December, and both my parents, my brother, and my sister and her family. I'm grateful to have resumed my friendship with Annemarie, best friend from childhood, indeed, to have had so many wonderful friendships in my life so far. I'm grateful for the freedom to do work that I love, for the time that Steve and I have to write, walk, and relax together, and for all the music I have enjoyed in my life. One of the first things I'll do in Vancouver is rejoin the Bach Choir, if they'll have me back. How I have missed that musical community since leaving Vancouver. And how many times the Choir has appeared in my dreams, symbolizing both the beauty and the sense of communal undertaking my soul hungers for so often in New York.

December 1st

A blustery, gray, peaceful first of December. Steve decided not to go into Manhattan for his Dialogue Meeting and we are both contentedly at work.

Again, I wonder, once the uncluttering has begun, what next? Do we look for a good cause to which we can devote time and energy? Do good deeds? Spend more time in creative pursuits? To what end do we simplify? Take friendship, for example. A topic that is always near and dear to my heart. How do we keep friendship free of unnecessary complexity?

Perhaps this involves saying what is really in our hearts, not what we think is going to make us appear wonderful, wise, and loving. But how difficult that is, and how risky. I do believe that the best way to simplify our communication with each other is to say what we think and feel as honestly as possible, so that the other person doesn't have to waste time wondering what we really mean and whether they should be trying to decode our words. Try to observe ourselves, what we do and how we make things more complicated than they have to be. How and where do I do that, I wonder?

(Do I really want to tell Sandra that I don't know, even after all our intense conversations, what our friendship is? That I feel disaffected at times, because she seems so casual about returning telephone calls and getting together? That I'm disappointed in our relationship, which began with such promise and excitement (on both our parts, I thought) and for which I had high hopes? Or do I simply accept it for what it is—with all its limitations? I don't know.)

Does simplicity in friendship mean having fewer friends so we can devote sufficient care and attention to each? I have friends in many parts of the world. Some are more essential to my happiness than others, and there are tides of intimacy and distance with each friend. Some go back two decades and longer. But why, I wonder, am I so often the one who desires a greater level of intimacy while the other person seems content with less? Some of my friends— especially those with children—have lives more complex than mine, I know. Still, it seems a shame that it's so often friendship that suffers when our lives become too crowded.

Twenty years ago, I assumed that when other people spoke of friendship, they meant more or less the same thing I did. Not anymore. The decade I have spent in New York, in particular, has shaken my basic assumptions, for example, that friends spend time together or at least speak on the telephone at length, that they take an active interest in each other's lives and well-being, and that honesty and self-disclosure deepen intimacy between people. It has been a hard lesson for me, sometimes painful. When I arrived in New York, I had the perhaps naive belief that the course of friendship was somewhat predictable. You meet someone who interests you and with whom you feel an emotional connection. They seem to feel the same way. You make plans to meet again, and do. Once you have done this a few times with warm feelings all around, you have struck up the beginning of a friendship.

Wrong. That's not necessarily the case at all, I discovered. What you have had is a series of discrete, enjoyable visits which don't necessarily add up to anything more. And, to my never-ending surprise, people seem to go on like this for years. Steve and I once heard ourselves described as "best friends" by a couple we typically see for dinner once or twice a year. I certainly never thought of them as our best friends. Is it just a New York pattern though? Even Steve, a lifelong New Yorker, doesn't fully understand it.

I used to swing between disappointment and anger over this syndrome, for want of a better term. Now, although I'm still puzzled and sometimes frustrated, mostly I'm resigned. I try to enjoy each social evening with no expectation that it might herald the beginning of a new friendship. And it has surely caused me to appreciate even more the ongoing friendships I've been blessed with till this day, with people—almost all are women—who return my eager interest in the large and small affairs of their lives, from one day and one year to the next. The regional peculiarities of friendship will no doubt remain one of the unresolved mysteries of my life in New York.

Perhaps, too, it's true that once we reach a certain age—probably somewhere in our thirties—the possibilities for striking up new friendships have diminished. Many people are coupled by then and it's much trickier for three or four people to hit it off than two. Often children are part of the picture, making casual visits much more complicated. The demands of juggling career and family are greatest during the thirties and forties and there's not much time left for meaningful outside relationships. I think this is especially true for those following a more traditional career trajectory, but it's certainly not limited to them. Even my friends who, like me, have chosen paths less traveled in their professional lives are often pulled in too many directions at once. And friendship becomes a luxury that can be infinitely deferred.

Perhaps I am simply out of sync with these times. Friendship, to me, is not expendable. It's not a luxury, but as essential to my well-being as clean air and healthy food. The people I care about deserve my love and attention, and I offer it freely and gladly, not out of duty or obligation. The immodest truth—I might as well admit it—is that I believe that I am a better friend than most people. Not because I am a better person, but because I value friendship more highly, give it greater importance in my life. While I have always had close friends in my life, I have to admit that too often I have been disappointed in friendship. Exactly what role I play in that, I'm not sure. Perhaps my expectations are simply too high, too idealistic. But I can't seem to shake them, try as I might. In this society and most, marriage is the privileged relationship; friendship doesn't even run a close second. But for me, it is one of the profound dimensions of human relationship and community, the source of great satisfaction and joy, and sometimes of anguish as well. I keep thinking of the wonderful final stanza of William Stafford's poem "A Ritual to Read to Each Other" that makes so beautifully clear the urgency of clarity and truthfulness between people:

> . . . For it is important that awake people be awake,
> or a breaking line may discourage them back to sleep;
> the signals we give—yes or no, or maybe—
> should be clear: the darkness around us is deep.[8]

When it comes to authentic communication, the darkness around us indeed is deep. And we are left feeling lonely.

December 4th

I haven't written here for several days now, probably because things are not at all simple at the moment. Our insurance company plans to penalize us for our involvement, last summer, in a multi-vehicle accident on the Belt Parkway that was in no way our fault. We were hit from behind, and although Steve was the only driver who managed not to hit anyone, we have been assessed an additional $800 a year in insurance premiums until an utterly false, trumped-up legal suit has been decided. They say they will refund the money if we are found not responsible. Guilty until proven innocent.

Mostly I feel angry at the injustice of being drawn into such craziness against our wills. Kafka was not so far off in his vision of a meaningless, self-perpetuating bureaucracy that sucks up people's life blood in order to justify its own existence! How ironic that we have chosen to see his work as an allegory of Communism even while Western capitalism exploits and sucks dry all in its path in its endless greed for profit.

December 5th

In the workshop last night I asked everyone to make a detailed list of simple pleasures in their lives. Here is my own.

- Walking on the boardwalk with Steve. Walking anywhere near water.
- Drinking café latté with a good friend.
- Writing when I'm alone in the house, on the couch with my beautiful tapestry cushions tucked all around me, Loreena McKennitt or Secret Garden playing in the background, and coffee and chocolate and lots of paper on the coffee table.

- Writing in a café, alone, comforted by the background noise and activity.
- Being invited into someone else's home and life. Looking at their bookshelves.
- Dancing to music with a good strong beat.
- Lying on the bed on a cold winter day and snuggling under a quilt with Steve or talking to a friend on the telephone.
- Sewing something creative, working carefully and in detail with my hands.
- Baking when I don't have to make anything in particular, inventing the recipe as I go along.
- Wrapping Christmas presents with Bach's "Christmas Oratorio" playing in the background.
- Beginning a new semester, when my hopes are high, the class looks promising, and I think that maybe this is what teaching is all about.
- Really connecting with a student with openness, mutual respect, and affection.
- Spending a day in Vancouver with an old friend whom I haven't seen in a long time and delving into everything that is important to us and knowing there won't be enough time.
- Going to a good movie with Steve, something we both like and can talk about time and time again, like *Wings of Desire* and *Antonia's Line.*
- Planning a new course, deciding on a reading list, reading the books, and planning out the classes.
- Spending quiet time with a friend where we aren't always talking, but reading, writing, resting, listening to music, or whatever the moment wants.
- Responding to someone who has written me a letter about *A Voice of Her Own,* knowing that somewhere

across the land, she walked into a bookstore, saw my
book and read it, and felt moved to write to me.
- Traveling on the Underground in London and feeling
that whole part of my past come alive again, only four
or five years long, and yet it seems like such a substan-
tial part of my life somehow.
- Buying fabrics, laces, and ribbons and imagining what I
might use them for.
- Planning and designing my gypsy skirts.
- Doing anything—or nothing—by candlelight.
- Peeling apples and chopping vegetables.
- Sewing something to give as a gift.

. . . And I could have continued. Who knew I had so many simple pleasures in my life!

December 9th

Today I want to write about making soup. In fact, this entry
could be called "In Praise of Soup" because it symbolizes so much
of what simple living means to me. It's easy to prepare and an efficient use of time; you can make a week's worth at once. It allows for
flexibility and creative experimentation; it's hard to make a serious
mistake. It's made of humble ingredients and you can use whatever
you have on hand. Nothing gets wasted, and it provides a wonderful
natural balance of ingredients. Not least, it's the perfect one-dish
meal to come home to on a cold winter night, as we have done for
years, with our ritual late Monday night soup suppers after class.

In *Composing a Life*, Mary Catherine Bateson described her mother's "ingenious formulas" for feeding the family and entertaining
guests. She tells us of her mother, the anthropologist, Margaret Mead,
"Her advice when I got married was to keep a soup pot simmering on
the stove so the house would smell of homecooking without too

much time spent in the kitchen—the symbol of loving effort without the hassle."[9]

This is the recipe I have developed over years of experimentation. It makes an enormous pot of hearty and satisfying soup that provides exactly the aroma Margaret Mead was after. It will stay fresh in the refrigerator for four or five days and freezes well.

Harvest Soup

1 large or 2 medium onions
several garlic cloves, or more if you like garlic
2 T. olive or canola oil
3 or 4 bay leaves
1/2 cup chopped parsley and/or fresh basil, or 1 T. dried
2 or 3 chicken or vegetable bouillon cubes
1/2 bunch of celery
1 lb. carrots
1 lb. potatoes (optional)
Approximately 10 cups in total of the following vegetables (use at least 3): cabbage, kale, Swiss chard or any other greens, green beans, peas, broccoli (including stems and leaves), turnips, asparagus, tomatoes, parsnips, squash (all varieties), spinach, Brussels sprouts, corn, cauliflower, leeks. You can also add beets, including greens, but these will turn your soup red. Whenever possible I use fresh vegetables, otherwise frozen. Add lentils, split peas, cooked soybeans or chickpeas, lima beans or other beans, especially if you don't add meat.
You can also add any combination of: brown rice or another whole grain. For a very thick consistency, use 1–2 cups barley. White rice doesn't need as much cooking time, so add it near the end. Bulgur and couscous can also be used; add them as you turn the

burner off at the end. You can add pasta instead of rice, but add it near the end, otherwise it gets soggy. Sometimes I cook it separately and ladle the soup over it, in individual bowls. You can also add leftover chopped chicken or turkey, ham, beef, or sausage. Or throw in a package of skinned chicken or turkey drumsticks to simmer along with the other ingredients.

Chop the onion and garlic, and sauté in a little oil in a large stock pot, until transparent.

Add chopped celery and carrots, bay leaf, and any other herbs and spices you like. (You can vary these each time you make the soup.)

Stir for a minute, then add three or four cups of cold water and the bouillon and bring to a boil.

Add the other vegetables and all other ingredients, cover with cold water, and let the soup simmer for 45 minutes or until the vegetables, rice, and legumes are soft but not mushy.

Add pasta near the end, because it will continue to cook even after you turn the burner off.

If you are adding cooked meat, wait until just before you turn the heat off.

Remember that all amounts are approximate and flexible. You can use more and less of whatever you have on hand. Begin with your own favorite chicken stock. I often add a large dollop of pesto sauce at the end for a rich flavor and color. This soup is substantial enough to be a meal in itself, but you can serve it with a crusty bread and butter or cheese, if you prefer.

What makes the recipe long are the creative options it offers. It's another case of using whatever is on hand to invent a different version each time.

December 18th

How dear this apartment seems every time I'm about to leave it. Mainly because it's where Steve and I have our life together— quietly, tenderly, and often so richly. One day I won't have to pack up and leave him in order to be "home for the holidays." If all goes well, it will only be three more Christmases like this, with my life so abruptly divided between everyday living and holidays. If I didn't have to go anywhere, if we were in Vancouver and could invite friends over for a meal, and go to a concert (or perhaps even sing in a concert), if we could relax over the semester break without having to pack our bags—how wonderful that would be.

Last night I browsed in *The Artist's Way* and came across the idea that when we find ourselves sorting through things, clearing out and uncluttering, we are making room for something new in our life. Julia Cameron writes, "One of the clearest signals that something healthy is afoot is the impulse to weed out, sort through, and discard old clothes, papers, and belongings. . . . By tossing out the old and unworkable, we make way for the new and suitable."[10] I am in such a phase now, wanting to get rid of things and clear some space, in more than one way. I would love to see my study bare and orderly, not piled high with books and papers, as it currently is. But what is the "new and suitable" that I am apparently preparing for?

December 19th,
in transit to British Columbia

In Chicago's airport, and I am too laden down with Christmas presents even to go into a café while I wait for my connecting flight to Vancouver. I don't want to do this again. It's madness.

What if we all agree to put gift-giving on hold for the next several years? What a relief it would be not to have to carry packages back and forth and we could all save shopping time and energy. Once we're back on the West Coast, we can discuss it again, decide what we want to do from then on. In the meantime, everyone would be spared the headache of Christmas shopping, and I'd get to travel light. I am going to suggest it to my family.

December 26th,
in Chilliwack, British Columbia, with Mum and Dad

Last night I discovered a copy of Thoreau's *Walden* among the hundreds of books I have stored in my parents' basement. Although Henry David Thoreau began his famous experiment in simple living in March of 1845, much of what he wrote rings true even now, more than a century and a half later, especially during the holiday season when most of us are frantic with social activity and there's so little time for the inner life.

Thoreau found that thirty days of physical labor a year were enough to supply all of his basic needs and the remaining eleven months could be used for other pursuits. "My greatest skill has been to want but little," he confidently proclaimed. "I am convinced, both by faith and experience, that to maintain one's self on this earth is not a hardship but a pastime, if we will live simply and wisely."[11] Perhaps that was an easier proposition in the mid-nineteenth century than it is now. Sound bites hadn't been invented and life moved at a slower pace. But I too am convinced "by faith and experience" that it is possible for us to rethink our lives and clear out much that is not essential. We create layer upon layer of unnecessary complexity in our lives through our unthinking desire to "have it all," our frantic, unquestioning rush to success, and our mistaken belief that *having* more equals *being* more.

I'm pleased to have a quiet day for myself, to gather my thoughts and contemplate how I would like the coming week to go. There is something peaceful about being at home with Mum and Dad, all of us puttering around with our individual tasks and projects, then meeting at mealtime.

Even during the years of greatest conflict between my parents and me when I was gradually breaking away from their evangelical Christian faith, I never scorned my roots. I have always been proud of coming from hardy central European stock, accustomed to hard work and possessing the ability to create something out of nothing. I see this reflected in my own quest for essentials. Even though my life with Steve in New York is quite different from anything they might have envisioned, it's a dimension of my heritage that I cherish. I know from lifelong experience that it doesn't take a great deal of money to have a wonderful quality of life. What it does take is imagination, ingenuity, and inventiveness. How rich I have felt over the years, simply because I have had time to think and reflect. Time to walk and converse, to read and write, to nurture friendship and make music, even though I haven't done it often enough in recent years.

December 29th

The blizzard continues, bringing its own kind of simplicity. There's very little to be done, with enormous piles of snow everywhere and more expected. A moment ago an announcement was made on the radio that, until further notice, no cars are allowed on the road except in emergencies. This is the harshest winter weather the West Coast has ever seen. No one is prepared, having been caught by surprise. The Vancouver International Airport is crammed with stranded passengers; fewer than one quarter of the scheduled flights are getting in and out. Here in Chilliwack, Evergreen Hall has been turned into a temporary shelter for stranded motorists and several hundred slept there last night, after being fed by Colonel Sanders and his crew. It's definitely a time to be grateful that we are warm and cozy in front of the fireplace with no need to head out into the bitter cold.

December 31st

The past few days I have felt restless, unfocused, at loose ends, mainly because things have not worked out according to plan. Steve will not be joining me on the West Coast after all, because the weather is still too unpredictable and the airports are in chaos. He could conceivably make the long flight here only to be told the plane can't land.

At all costs, a part of me wants to be productive, it seems. Instead of fretting over the upset in our plans, why can't I just accept the extra time gratefully, read in front of the fireplace, and think ahead to my workshop in Vancouver next Tuesday? If life hands you the lemons of isolation, make the lemonade of solitude. Truth is, I don't like having my carefully laid plans thwarted, and they surely were this time. But I'll try to do better from here on in. One disappointing holiday is not the end of the world.

January 6th,
in Vancouver

Happy New Year! The snow stopped falling and I am finally in Vancouver. Yesterday I discussed simple living with Angela and Jean over breakfast. They laughed at the idea of getting off the fast track because they, too, feel they never got on it. Their apartment is light and airy, minimalist. They have simple furniture in neutral tones. Nothing is superfluous. Angela showed me their personal archives, consisting of more than a dozen large boxes that hold personal documents from over the years. Everything else gets tossed out immediately. I can't be that ruthless. But I can indeed take a lesson from them and throw out much more than I presently do.

January 9th,
en route back to New York

I have lived away from Vancouver for fourteen years now, averaging two visits a year. It's not always easy to live a double life, although at the best of times, it can be wonderful. I have managed to keep friendships alive and flourishing in B. C. while also creating a rich life over time with Steve in New York. All in all I've managed to do it pretty successfully, I think, albeit with considerable stress and heartache at times.

Like most people, I've been faced with a great many conflicts. I want to be with Steve, but also spend a lot of time with my own family on the other shore. I want to live in a beautiful place where the landscape feeds my soul, but here I am, in New York, urban capital of the world. I want to do work I find meaningful, but I've got to earn a living. I love to be with people, but I need solitude to write. We want to save money, but airfare to Vancouver is expensive. I want to have a gracious home and cook tasty and nutritious food, but not be a slave to housework. I crave intellectual stimulation, but am drawn to create useful and beautiful things with my hands. I want to have it all, to fit everyone and everything I love into my life.

So, given these external coordinates of my life, how can I live simply? How to simplify travel, for example. Pack minimally, and leave basic year-round items of clothing and staple toiletries in B. C. Plan travel well in advance, in order to take advantage of seat sales and have time to organize other events in New York and Vancouver around my travel dates. Keep in mind what I'm going home for—to spend time with family and friends in a quiet and meaningful way—and not try to fit in too much else. What I really long for is leisurely walks by the ocean and long conversations in cafés with friends—not fancy dinners, concerts, or theatre. Plan to do some sewing that I don't make time for in New York. Take advantage of the open time and space, and indulge my homebody self.

January 13th

Back in New York since last night, I'm gradually getting back into things. I'm keeping "re-entry" soft and slow, not trying to do everything at once.

I've been thinking about simplicity in relation to my work: teaching, writing, and running the workshops. It seems I'm beginning to extend it into every area of my life. Since I'm feeling a little overwhelmed by the amount of paperwork facing me, I want to try to streamline and throw out as much as possible, to keep my head clear. I lack working space. My study is piled so high with books and paper that I've been working at the dining room table.

Last October 14th, just before I began this journal, I asked the *I Ching,* "What project should I turn to next?" The answer I got was: "Initial Difficulty" followed by "Biting Through," and the final message was, "Difficulties dispensing benefits on a great scale. Persistence in small things—good fortune. Persistence in great things—evil."

If I relate this to the Women's Journal Workshop, it suggests I should continue as I have been doing: Keep focusing on the quality and depth of my workshops and forget about becoming known or recognized in the journal world. Since I don't even want a high-profile life and everything that accompanies it, I'm better off proceeding in the quiet, personal way that characterizes the journal, doing things as thoughtfully as I can.

It takes great energy to keep rethinking the values we are handed—bigger is better, fame and prestige are good, success is externally defined—and to keep asking, "Is this really what's most important to me? Is this how I want to live?" It reminds me of a wonderful passage in Etty Hillesum's diary, where she wrote,

> Much of what I do is mere imitation, springs from a sense of duty or from preconceived notions of how people should behave. The only certainties about what is right and wrong are those which spring from sources deep inside oneself.[12]

The difficulty in these relentlessly extroverted times, it seems to me, lies in getting in touch with those sources deep inside ourselves. For that we need time and solitude, and a bedrock faith in our own innate wisdom, even when it goes against every prevailing trend and tendency.

January 14th

These days of brilliant cold sunshine and no commitments are so precious. Silent companionship—Steve is in his study—and I'm working on many things at once. Body and soul are at peace.

I began rereading Anne Morrow Lindbergh's *Gift from the Sea*, amazed by how thoroughly relevant it is, perhaps even more so than when she wrote it in 1955. She described so beautifully the many tugs and pulls women experience, now, as then.

> To be a woman is to have interests and duties, raying out in all directions from the central mother-core, like spokes from the hub of a wheel. The pattern of our lives is essentially circular. We must be open to all points of the compass; husband, children, friends, home, community; stretched out, exposed, sensitive like a spider's web to each breeze that blows, to each call that comes. How difficult for us, then, to achieve a balance in the midst of these contradictory tensions, and yet how necessary for the proper functioning of our lives.[13]

Although she felt that having a husband and five children made it next to impossible for her to simplify her life, Anne longed for solitude to find her own still center. My life is different from hers. Apart from our teaching responsibilities, Steve and I have few time-consuming obligations. We are both somewhat allergic to official groups and organizations. Right or wrong, this ends up saving us a great deal of time. Alas, it's not always time wisely used. We often walk after dinner, but we also watch too much television at times, instead of singing or spending the evening in other creative pursuits. That's something I want to work on.

But she's right. We do spend most of our lives trying to create a satisfying balance of work, the companionship of family and friends, creative pursuits, solitude, and personal projects of various kinds. It's rare that everything comes together in an ideal harmony of sorts. At any given time we may feel that there's too much of one thing, not enough of another.

Here in New York I have ample personal time and solitude, but not enough intimate companionship, apart from Steve. I derive great satisfaction from teaching and writing, homemaking, and creating my workshops, but I haven't been making music, a dimension of my life conspicuous by its absence over the past five years. I realize just how great a loss this is when we go to a concert and I experience phantom pain, as if from a limb removed long ago but still astrally present. And of course, children are lacking: my own or others I could dearly love, including Stefan and Chelsea, my nephew and niece. I have no family on the East Coast; a double-edged sword. No burdens, no blessings. And the landscape here does not nourish my soul like the West Coast panorama of mountains and ocean. How I long to get back to my soul's home.

January 16th

The relationship between inner and outer simplicity—Steve and I were discussing it yesterday. Either, on its own, cannot be complete. How can my inner life be serene if my external life is chaotic and overburdened? Conversely, my life in the workplace can't be simple if my psyche is filled with unresolved fears and conflicts. How do we bring the two into harmony? In his writing, Steve has described a "Möbius strip reality" in which outer and inner experience are completely interdependent, where "the conceptual and the experiential can flow into one another without interruption."[14] That's surely what we need if we are to experience inner and outer simplicity as part of a single whole. But how to enact this in our lives?

Walking from the ferry terminal up to the Angelika cinema last night, I realized again how much I *don't* want to live like this. The aggressive noise and pollution shock my system every time we go into Manhattan and leave a stronger impression, on balance, than the exhilaration and excitement of the city. I found myself irritated by the thronging hordes, my nerves on edge because of the relentless noise. I wondered how living like that, year after year, would affect one's central nervous system over time. One would have to develop blocking mechanisms in order to survive; no wonder people don't look at each other, much less smile, in these streets.

No doubt it would feel different if we lived in an interesting neighborhood like the Upper West Side and began to think of it as our home, to know the local stores and coffee shops and grow accustomed to the constant high energy and action. Perhaps we'd even grow to love it. Somehow I doubt it, though. I need something more pastoral, a whole lot more green, a vista that feeds both eye and soul, even more than I need Zabar's Delicatessen and the wonderful cappuccino bars nearby.

January 17th

It occurred to me while I was out walking today that what I'm contemplating is something like "simplicity through the back door." Perhaps the most important dimension of simplifying is *doing one thing at a time*. "Mindfulness," as the Zen Buddhists and New Age books refer to it. It's the best "technique" for simple living that I know of. None of the practical dimensions seem to make much sense if the deepest, truest level of the soul is not engaged. If our yearning for simplicity doesn't resonate on that level, what's the point? I want to be very aware of *why* I do what I do. This mode of attentiveness is a little easier for me now than it used to be—there are fewer distractions.

One of the unexpected benefits of having passed forty, for example, is that I don't subconsciously live as much in anticipation of the next admiring glance, the next compliment, the next chance to be thought beautiful, as I did in my twenties and thirties. Now I can dwell more deeply in the present moment, simply offering my attention to whatever it holds. Life is no longer what will happen tomorrow or next year; it's fully underway right now. Etty Hillesum describes this realization so beautifully in her journal. On March 21, 1941, she wrote,

> In the past I would live chaotically in the future, because I refused to live in the here and now. . . . Sometimes I had the certain if rather undefined feeling that I would "make it" one day, that I had the capacity to do something extraordinary, and at other times the wild fear that I would "go to the dogs" after all. I now realise why. I simply refused to do what needed to be done, what lay right under my nose. . . . Before, I always lived in anticipation, I had the feeling that nothing I did was the "real" thing, that it was all a preparation for something else, something "greater," more "genuine." But that feeling has

dropped away from me completely, I live here-and-now,
this minute, this day, to the full, and life is worth living.[15]

Etty learned this much earlier in her short life than I. I was into my thirties before I began slowly to recognize what she already saw so clearly at twenty-five. Perhaps her desperate circumstances sped up her learning process. Or maybe she was just wiser and more mature than I, and recognized early on that "Life is not a dress rehearsal." Don't sit around waiting for "the real thing" because this is it.

January 20th

How does the role of money figure into my search for simplicity? There is a big distinction between thinking of money as food on the table and regarding it as a guarantee of a certain standard of living. These are very different conceptions of what money is for.

It brings back fond memories of life at Willy G. in the mid-eighties. I was living on very little money—my £35 a week had to cover everything from food and clothing to books and travel. Tuesday was always my night tending the small wine bar outside the common room. For four hours of relaxed and sociable work I received the grand sum of £8. Even though that was a mere pittance, it paid for half a week's groceries. I was happy to earn it in such an agreeable way and to have a legitimate excuse not to work on my thesis one night each week. (Not that I worked on all the other nights; I just felt guilty about not working.) I also earned a little money by "child-minding," as it is called in England. Sometimes I really didn't feel inclined to deal with cranky little ones while their better-off-than-I parents went to the opera. But even six or eight pounds extra income made such a difference.

I ate simply but very well. Lots of fruit, salad, pasta, and the wonderful wholegrain sunflower bread from Crank's Natural Foods

Bakery that was the closest thing to Mum's bread I ever found in London. I also fell in love with Indian food during those years, when my Jamaican friend Taniya and her friend Davine, from South Africa, taught me to make chickpea, lamb, and chicken curries, pungent with ginger and fresh coriander.

I was very happy. I had a wide variety of fascinating friends and acquaintances from all over the world, and my large sunny room overlooked the leafy green of Mecklenburgh Square, on the same property where Virginia Woolf's house had stood before it was blown up during the war. I had my Melitta coffeemaker (inherited from Gabi and Jörg when they packed up to return to Frankfurt), free access to practice rooms with pianos where I could sing—and all of London before me. Every Saturday morning I baked apricot oatmeal or banana walnut muffins and slipped half a dozen through the milk window in Prue and John's little apartment just around the corner.

Once a week I walked to the local health food store for my weekly pound of garbanzo beans (25 pence), brown rice, figs, and dates, and left with a heavy bag, five or six pounds in total. Then I'd stop at the greenmarket behind Oxford Street and pick up carrots, potatoes, apples, and bananas, so heavy that I could hardly carry my shopping bag back to the residence.

And I didn't eat out. I simply couldn't afford to. Amazingly I did not even feel hard done by. After I met Steve, he'd take me out for dinner every Saturday night and it was such a treat. One evening we went to an Indian restaurant and I introduced him to curry, which began his love of Indian food as well. On Sunday nights I'd cook pasta for him on the little two-burner stove in our communal kitchen.

I thought I had everything I needed to be happy, and more. I was never cold or hungry or lonely. I walked everywhere and was fit and healthy. If I felt sad or depressed, there was always a friend to talk to: Laurence or Françoise, Prue or Annemarie, Janet or Gabi.

Never—before or since—have I been so rich in intimate friendship. There's no denying how much I miss that sense of communal relatedness. I knew of course that this would end with my final year of student life. I just didn't comprehend how big the gulf would be between the life of a doctoral student in London and that of a part-time college professor on Staten Island. What a shock that was to my emotional system.

Yesterday I looked at various books on simplicity at Barnes & Noble on the Upper West Side. I can't think of a nicer way to spend an afternoon than to settle in, on the carpet if necessary, with a stack of books and several hours of free time. You can even take the books into the café with you—a small consolation, at least, for the sad fact that they have put Shakespeare & Company in New York and so many other independent booksellers all across the country out of business.

Most of the books I saw seem to equate simplicity either with frugality, on the one hand, or with purely spiritual concerns, on the other. You find them in the "Personal Finance" and "Spirituality" sections; outer and inner simplicity get split again. But what interests me is precisely how they work together to make a whole life, as an expression of the person's integrity. "Integrity" stems from the Latin *integer*, as does "entire." *Integrare*, the verb, means to make whole and complete. That is how I want my life to be.

January 21st

An open day stretches out before me. There's nothing I *must* do; plenty that I *want* to. We're heading over to Clove Lake Park this afternoon to walk in glorious sunshine. I'll stop at the bookstore for the new film book by Molly Haskell to see if it's appropriate for my Women's Studies class. We got out of bed at eight this morning, had coffee and corn muffins, and proceeded to our studies. I rang Nancy to ask how the move to their newly purchased condo went on

Saturday, before sitting down to work. Concern or procrastination? Maybe a little of both.

After our walk Steve will pick up our mail at the College while I make an enormous pot of soup for dinner and the coming week. Tonight I want to begin rereading *Sense and Sensibility* for my "Woman as Hero" class and work on Nellie's quilt, or bake some peanut butter cookies. Perhaps we'll sing. Music is almost completely missing from our lives right now—one of the unresolved mysteries of my life in New York. I'm counting on our eventual move west to inspire me to get back to it.

So—what is there to simplify here? Most people I know would look at our life together and say we are fortunate to have so little red tape, so few involved complications. We don't own a home, so we have no responsibility for maintenance or repairs. We don't have complicated childcare arrangements; Steve's children are basically grown up. We're both reasonably healthy. We have a steady income. We're able to get by with one car. We love what we do. We have friends. We can travel if we want to, and we have our "three year plan" for Vancouver. We don't place great importance on material possessions. We're saving as much money as we can and expect to achieve a modest degree of financial independence in three to five years. I suppose we're fortunate to have fairly basic needs and not feel deprived by living below our means.

There's no question that a lot of this is a result of conscious choice. We surely could have frittered a lot more money away on recreational spending and expensive restaurants if we were so inclined. But in the back of my mind there is always the idea that money equals freedom, and that more than anything else, I want to be free to write, sing, plan workshops, and explore other creative possibilities. I love eating out, but it doesn't have to be in four-star restaurants. If the company is good, curry or a dish of pasta is just fine.

At home, we'd just as soon eat my hearty soup as steak, especially with all of the recent stories about contaminated beef. The two huge pots simmering on the stove at the moment—about twenty quarts—will provide many satisfying suppers, especially on nights that we both teach late. This will be a delicious batch, full of barley and split peas, onions, carrots and cabbage, celery, bay leaf, squash, turnips, corn and potatoes, and the organic beef sausage I brought back from B. C. And the whole thing probably costs under ten dollars to make.

Well then, is cooking in large quantities in order to save time and energy and eat healthful suppers with a minimum of fuss an example of what I mean by simple living? The topic continues to draw me in with its complexity and elusiveness.

January 22nd

I read most of May Sarton's new book, *At Eighty-Two,* last night. Her journals engage the reader because they are intimate and personal, revealing the ordinariness of her life, full of joys and sorrows, small and large. Sarton writes so openly about her depression and loneliness (if not, it turns out, about all other dimensions of her personal life!) that it allows me to be frank as well about my own sporadic envy of more successful writers, my unhappiness with how the publication of my first book was handled, my ups and downs regarding friendships, and my never-ending stream of petty grievances about assorted matters!

Now that Margot Peters, her authorized biographer, has cast doubt on the veracity of her journals, there will doubtless be a major reevaluation of her work, but the emotional truth expressed in her journals will survive, I feel, just as with the *Diaries* of Anais Nin. Publishing a private journal that was not intended for publication, as in Nin's case, is a tricky affair at best. How to narrate one's inner life without compromising the privacy of others concerned. Nin did it by showing people what she'd written about them and obtaining their permission. But she also omitted huge chunks of her diary text, and that has to mean it's a partial truth at best. Now that the "unexpurgated" version has appeared in print, we have some sense of just how much was left out and how those omissions affect our overall sense of her life.

What about inner simplicity? Perhaps it consists of gaining more and more clarity about what is essential, staying aware and conscious, and observing one's thinking. Trying to say exactly what one means. Not for effect, to impress or smooth things over, but simply in order to communicate as clearly and honestly as possible. How to do this in a loving fashion?

Maybe it also means not allowing oneself to be seduced by false alternatives, or veering off one's path. Staying mindful of the many distractions out there which tempt one first this way, then that, always with the promise of some new momentary gratification, so that we end up feeding false hungers while our genuine yearning for meaning goes unaddressed.

It's not easy, though. The pressure to want and have it all is great. It isn't fashionable to keep old things—cherished, worn, and loved— for long periods of time. Rapid turnover, the built-in obsolescence of material things, that's what has been in vogue for several decades now. More, faster, newer, and "better." This economy is driven by our thoughtless, excessive, and addictive consumption. It takes careful discrimination to determine whether one needs the new sweater, the new television set or computer—or simply craves it, out of greed and habit.

January 23rd

I'm still thinking about inner simplicity, and the vivid image comes to me of someone taking a dozen long, slow breaths in a peaceful setting and tuning in to the body's felt sense. It's a meditative state wherein we try to quiet the mind's usual nonstop chatter and sink down into something that is bedrock, essential, constant. And what we discover below our surface desires and impulses is the living, breathing body, the cells of our organism that rejoice at simply being alive. Everything else is added on: our neuroses, assorted resentments, and the constant need for ego reinforcement. I know this is true for me.

When people talk about simplifying—and there seems to be much discussion in the air—I often wonder how many of them actually know what their own dearest values and priorities are. If they don't know that, how will they know what to simplify back from, and down to? If simplifying is to mean something beyond merely getting rid of old clutter, it demands a high degree of discrimination. What is essential in our lives, and what can be cleared out? What is real and vital today, and what is old habitual practice that can be shed, making room for something new?

And what about time? What is it for? How do we determine what is time "well spent" and "wasted" time? There are so many implicit assumptions in those words, as if we all agreed on what has value, what deserves our time, and what does not.

Growing up, it was clear to me that any time I was off in a quiet corner reading, I was "wasting time." Time well used brought concrete results: a counter covered with steaming freshly baked bread or two dozen jars of canned cherries. At the end of the day, there was always something tangible to show for it. This was obviously not the case with reading! Looking back, I can see how that must have bothered my parents, who'd arrived in Canada with nothing to their names. Time was not just money; it was survival. A roof over their heads—there was no heating during the first few winters and the water froze overnight in pails in the kitchen—and food on the table. What practical purpose did reading serve?

But I could never get enough. Two or three times a week I'd check out six books, the maximum allowed, at the Chilliwack Public Library. I couldn't wait to get into the adult section, with its tantalizing promise of "real" literature. Finally the librarian, who recognized me, granted me access at the age of twelve, two years early. I spent many blissful hours there after school, pleading homework. My parents must have wondered how they'd gotten a child like that, since neither shared my passion for books.

Even in my adult years, I've had to justify—to myself, now—the hours spent reading. Often I fight the guilty urge to leap up and do something more "useful"—to grade student essays, clean, cook, bake, or sew—anything that produces a visible result. That conditioning runs deep. But I feel this less urgently now than a decade ago.

I read differently too: more selectively, and at a more measured pace. Perhaps it has to do with finally accepting that I will never read every book I want to during my lifetime. The result is that I'm reading fewer books than in the past, but the books I do read work more deeply within and on me. The work of Jungian analyst Marion Woodman, for example, stays with me long after I read it, resonating in my body, nourishing my soul, providing food for thought and inspiration for my own writing and workshops. When I first discovered Marion's work, it seemed I had stumbled across a new language and syntax, one which my mind was not sure it understood. My body, on the other hand, prickled with excitement, reverberating to the tuning fork of her words with an almost shocking sense of recognition and familiarity. Reading on, I felt comforted and nourished, as if some hidden hunger were at long last being satisfied.

But, to return to the original question: Why do I, why do we feel we have to "use" time productively, toward the achievement of some external goal, instead of *dwelling* within it?

Sometimes I spend quiet, graceful days at home, moving easily and almost without noticing it from one thing to the next. There is a natural flow to the movement; body and soul are in harmony. I may not be doing anything of earthshaking importance but I am serene. I don't fight with unrealistic expectations of how much I ought to get done. I just keep breathing, moving, resting in time. As if a quiet melody is singing within my body, weaving everything together in an unbroken flow of rich contrapuntal contentment. As if I were living in a Bach fugue.

I love that experience of feeling myself inside the moment, which is, at the same time, an obliviousness to time passing. The experience is one of richness and equanimity, of fullness and sufficiency, of total absorption and immersion in the task at hand. How to experience that flow more often is the question.

January 25th

And now I must prepare myself—body, mind, and soul—to begin teaching again in less than a week. I want to have a good semester: to teach with an open heart, and to offer my students something genuine and substantial. Frustrated with the Journal class last term, I want to put it behind me now, and start out fresh. I want to be productive, to enjoy everything I do, from teaching and exercise to cleaning and my other chores. *All of it.*

January 30th

Each time the Women's International Writing Guild newsletter, *Network*, arrives, I feel the urge to jump up and be more active, visible, and self-promoting. Reading other members' reports of their professional activities makes me wonder if I should be doing more to publicize my book and workshop. By not jumping into the thick of things, I leave myself on the fringe.

And yet, that's where I like to be. Why does a part of me seek to be in the forefront of attention? Where does that urge come from? If that is truly where I want to be, I'd have done just about everything in my life to date differently. I'd be making conference proposals all over the place and making myself as visible as possible, instead of hiding my light under a bushel. "Your women's writing circle is the best kept secret on Staten Island," I have been told more than once. Indeed. But not by design. I simply had no interest in doing publicity, in selling myself or my workshop.

My refusal to jump on that particular bandwagon, I feel intuitively, is part of my desire to live simply. I'm reluctant to squander my limited life energy. I'm even over-protective of my solitude at times and can end up feeling cabin-feverish and isolated. The truth is, I've always been something of an *Einzelgänger,* just like Steve. We both march to the beat of a different drummer and sometimes that leaves us marching alone.

But if I really believe that my gift and calling are to work with women in small groups, perhaps my task is simply to continue the work I have been doing. Maybe I should not worry about whether I'm doing impressive workshops in the world beyond our living room or whether my name is becoming known in the journal world. We're easily persuaded, I think, that fame and public visibility are accurate measures of the impact we are making, but something tells me this is not quite true.

Jungian analyst Helen Luke, quoting the *I Ching,* has something wonderfully relevant to say about this. She writes, "When the quiet power of a [wo]man's own character is at work, the effects produced are right. All those who are receptive to the vibration of such a spirit will then be influenced." Then, quoting Confucius, she adds, "The superior [wo]man abides in [her] room. If [her] words are well spoken, [she] meets with assent at a distance of more than a thousand miles. How much more then from near by!"[16] What evocative words. But it's an ongoing struggle not to crave the praise and appreciation of people who might find my book and me wonderful. There's nothing simple about seeking recognition, or even about wanting to be admired for *not* seeking it. One really has to be clear about one's path to remain faithful to it. Even with the sincere desire, it's so difficult to grasp the truth about oneself. That blindspot again.

January 31st

Taking stock of my financial life so far, at the ripe old age of forty-three I have never owned a car or a home or paid a mortgage. The most costly thing I've ever purchased was my computer in 1992. I don't spend money on jewelry, clothing, or furniture, and I have never been in debt, except for a small student loan which I paid off with the first money I earned. I've never owned a credit card, although I now share Steve's. My only regret, really, is that I didn't open a retirement savings plan during the years I worked full-time, 1973–74 and 1978–79, because that money would have grown exponentially by now, and would be a tidy sum by the time I'm sixty-five. But people in general were not as financially savvy then, and retirement savings were really the last thing on my mind. My only thought during those years was to save a few thousand dollars and travel.

I have always lived very well on minimal income, clear that my greatest priorities were time, independence, and freedom of movement. As I looked around at the grinding nine to five options available, none seemed worth sacrificing the best hours of my life for. And even now, looking back, I'm not sorry. I regret only that I wasn't more courageous in my choices, bolder in my adventures, more outrageous in my creative endeavors, and generally more willing to take risks. But never mind; it's not too late. Who wants to wait until I'm an old woman to wear purple? I want to wear it now!

February 7th

We watched part of the movie *Gandhi* on television last night. I was reminded that Gandhi wove his own cloth from Indian cotton—rather than buy imported English fabric—in order to show solidarity with the desperately poor Indian farmers. This is just one example of his attempt to live consistently and with uncompromising integrity.

I don't know what a simplified wardrobe would be for me now. Several summers ago it was half a dozen Indian skirts and matching T-shirts. Several simplicity books suggest maintaining a very basic wardrobe in just one or two colors, but that would never work for me. I love color too much, and the Indian skirts were gaudy and gorgeous.

For now, I'm simply not buying any clothes. I have an abundance of everything I need, including several dresses and jackets I've never even worn. I'll wear what I have, and gradually figure out how to unclutter my wardrobe. Meanwhile, I'll keep sorting through my closets and donate everything I don't wear to the local shelter for battered women. I'll ask myself, Is this traveling to Vancouver with us? If not, I'll give it away or throw it out. Now.

February 10th

The core of simplicity, I believe, is getting clear what is most important to us, both in the course of our daily lives and over the long run. But this is not easy. How do we tell the difference between what we feel we *ought* to want and our true, often deeply suppressed, passionate wants and needs? How do we distinguish among our unchecked desires, what we have been taught to want and reach for, and what the soul really requires to blossom and expand?

I think it has to do with bringing the inner self and the social self into harmony and alignment, which begins with being able to differentiate between them. I'm reminded of Christa Wolf's citation of the German dramatist Georg Büchner: "When the masks come off, 'Do the faces come off with them?'"[17] Do we know the difference between our social persona and our soul's truth?

It takes constant vigilance to stay conscious of this never-ending dialogue in our lives. Often we get so caught up in the practical demands of day-to-day living that even to ask such questions seems self-indulgent. But I don't think it is. It's one of the most important questions we can ask ourselves. Because, conscious or not, it's the driving force that propels our lives. When it remains unconscious, we live out the answer in our daily lives, in the choices we make compulsively, time and time again. If the driving force is ambition, we do whatever it takes. If it's the pursuit of money, we arrange our lives accordingly. Whatever it is, it rules our lives. We cannot afford to be blind to this, because our very lives are at stake.

February 16th

Searching for simplicity is like walking around a lake. You know you're looking at the same body of water no matter where you are, but it looks different depending on where you stand.

Discussing it with Nellie on the telephone the other day, I thought again that at the very heart of the desire to simplify there must be a period of introspection and soul-searching during which we ask ourselves: What is my purpose in life, and how is it reflected in the way I use my time? When am I most myself? If income and external obligations were not factors in my decision, what would I choose to do with my days?

Not that asking these questions causes everything miraculously to fall into place, but internally, things do begin to shift and become clearer. Often this involves sorting out what we've learned to accept as the external signs of a successful life (a family, a large home, money, professional recognition, cars, vacations, and a certain standard of living) from what might offer us genuine fulfillment and satisfaction (time for creative pursuits, satisfying relationships, meaningful study, physical activity, travel, and so on).

Sometimes we don't even realize that there's a discrepancy. Fearful of disturbing a more or less acceptable life pattern, too busy to acknowledge our own unhappiness, and unwilling to name the underlying sense of despair and emptiness that gnaws at us from time to time, we go through our lives on automatic pilot, sure that the twin engines of habit and ambition will prevent us from straying too sharply off course.

For many reasons it behooves us to remain acquiescent, indeed unconscious. But I'm convinced that if we genuinely yearn for simpler and more meaningful lives—and mean by this more than ridding our living space of material clutter—then we have to keep reaching for ever-increasing awareness of the terms on which we actually live our lives. In what direction does the greater part of our life energy flow? Is that in accordance with our best understanding of our life's purpose? If not, do we want to acknowledge the inconsistency and make some changes?

May Sarton said it very well in the following passage:

> The price of being oneself is so high and involves so much ruthlessness toward others (or what looks like ruthlessness in our duty-bound culture) that very few people can afford it. Most people swallow the unacceptable because it makes life so much easier.[18]

February 17th

Yesterday I made an enormous pot of meat sauce. It took me several hours to brown seven pounds of lean ground sirloin and chop celery, onions, peppers, carrots, mushrooms, and parsley. I threw in some organic lentils and soybeans from the freezer for extra nutrition and fiber. Now the counter is covered with more than a dozen pints, enough to last us into the fall. And it's delicious. Cooking like this frees up so much time. It means many twenty-minute dinners that will involve only cooking pasta and chopping up a few fresh vegetables or fruits for a salad. How did we ever get by without a deep-freezer for all those years?

Meat Sauce

2 T. olive or canola oil
3 lbs. lean or extra lean ground beef
1–2 large onions
several garlic cloves
salt and pepper
1 tsp. fresh or dried oregano, basil, parsley, mixed Italian
    herbs, as desired
1 small can tomato paste and 1 large can crushed toma-
    toes, OR 1 jar of prepared tomato sauce

Sauté onions and garlic in oil until transparent. Add beef, separating any chunks that form. Stir so it browns thoroughly. Add tomato paste, crushed tomatoes, and herbs, and simmer for half an hour at low heat, stirring occasionally. Add salt and pepper to taste. Serve with any shape and size of pasta, and sprinkle lots of freshly ground Parmesan cheese on top. This makes a wonderful lasagna sauce as well.

    * You can also add chopped mushrooms, zucchini, eggplant, celery, carrots, if desired.

February 18th

Last night I finished Nellie's birthday quilt. I felt a little rushed because I want to get it to her for her March 1st birthday, but it turned out beautifully. There are squares cut from fabric left over from her high school choir blouse and from scraps of dresses and skirts I've made for her, and for my mother, niece, and aunt over the years. I wish all of the fabric in the quilt held memories, but alas, we gave away so much during a big clean-out a few years ago when it seemed no one had any use for it.

I wanted to give Nellie something special for her fortieth birthday. She and Ken already have a large quilt that I made for them several years ago, but this one is especially for her. It's a smaller quilt, made for cozy warmth on a cold, gray afternoon spent snuggled up on the sofa with a cup of hot chocolate, a journal, and a good book. At a time when our relationship is changing in a way that leaves both of us feeling vulnerable, I hope she feels enveloped in the warmth of my love whenever she uses it.

February 23rd

I love Sundays like this. Steve has a meeting in Connecticut and I have the house to myself for several hours. I rang Maureen in Montreal, and we spoke for more than an hour, one of our intense "checking in on the state of your life" conversations. We understand each other's verbal shorthand so well after more than two decades of friendship. This afternoon I want to do some teaching preparation, think about my upcoming workshop series on "Journal Writing and the Art of Simple Living," bake some cakes to put into the freezer, write a letter or two, and perhaps take a walk, in the middle of it all. When I feel light-hearted and optimistic, a day like this has a sense of great freedom about it. There is more to do than I can possibly fit in, and all of it provides satisfaction in the doing.

. . . 4 p.m.

I just threw out—with a heavy heart—about three-quarters of all the cards and letters I've received in New York since my arrival in 1988. Each one represents a loving impulse shared, and it's difficult to discard it. Still, since I can't imagine taking them to Vancouver with me, what's the point of hanging on to them when I'm so short of space for my current projects?

And I suppose that this correspondence represents the past, not the present, of those relationships, in any case. It served its purpose the day I received it, and now it's time to let it go and create more space for the present. There will be more loving moments, many I hope. I'd rather write a note to someone today than reread what they wrote me many years ago. It's one less form of clutter in my life. But I did save one piece from each friend, as a memento.

February 24th

The question I keep coming back to: What do I mean by simplicity, and how can I best embody it in my life? I don't mean austerity or asceticism; I'm too much a sensualist for that. What I want is a harmony of intention where one is guided by a single all-embracing purpose in life, something that one never forgets or loses sight of for long; that, even while slowly evolving over the years, still remains constant and recognizable. Perhaps it's something like this that people mean when they refer to "God's will," or to having a "pure heart." That this is essentially a spiritual quest, is clear to me. It involves the quest for *essence,* some core of meaning and value that remains constant throughout a lifetime and perhaps beyond. Perhaps it's what some refer to as the quest for the essential Self, and what Jung meant by individuation.

February 26th

Helen Luke (quoting Meister Eckhart) writes, "'Wisdom consists in doing the next thing you have to do. Doing it with your whole heart and finding delight in doing it.' And that is the simplicity of the feminine values. You stay with the moment, the small thing." In old age, Luke says, this comes easily. You don't have a choice, because "you can't do anything else as the old, aging body is apt to teach you!"[19]

What a far cry from the way we normally do things, disdaining what seems uninteresting or unworthy of our time, always preoccupied with the next task, which seems more significant and of greater consequence. And so we miss the fullness and reality of the present moment. Because we deem it trivial, we are not present to it in an embodied way. The old scale of measurement and value rules once again and we pronounce it a waste of time. And it is always our loss.

Maybe this also explains the chronic discontent so rampant in our society. Never really present, we're always off somewhere else in imagination, wanting something more, something better, faster, more rewarding than what we have. I know that I am guilty of this when I denigrate our life on Staten Island and hungrily anticipate our move to Vancouver. Most often I feel it can't come soon enough for me, and I have to stop and remind myself not to wish away these precious days and years. Each one is unique and irreplaceable, but I have to keep reminding myself of that, all too often.

March 1st

Walking back from the library this afternoon with *The Poverty of Affluence* under my arm, I thought about how often we bemoan our busy lives and complain about the lack of time to do what we really want, all the while deriving secret satisfaction from being so heavily booked. It's fashionable to be "too busy." In our society it's essential to be seen as someone whose time is valuable and who must therefore be important. It's not good strategy to have time conspicuously available at short notice, or to openly enjoy days without the packed schedule that signifies a life of consequence.

From time to time I find myself falling into this mind frame. When asked how I am, it's so easy to reply, "I'm fine. Busy, but otherwise well." Behind this automatic response, I suppose, is the feeling that if I'm not busy, I surely *ought* to be, if I want to be seen as a valuable member of society. We equate busyness with productivity and productivity with financial success, but oddly, with moral virtue as well.

There are, however, times when I'm *not* busy, times when I have complete control over my schedule and can do just what I like. And sometimes I do feel the temptation to take on more responsibility, accomplish more, and to be more visible. "I *should* do more high-profile workshops; I *should* have a full-time academic job; I *should* network more and be more strategic as far as marketing my book is concerned; *should* have appeared on television by now; *should* have another book out already." So the internal voices admonish me. But there's a stubborn part of me that won't be bullied, even by myself.

I don't want to buy blindly into the belief that busyness equals importance, just to satisfy my ego's need for recognition. I want to stay conscious of the seductions of productivity and measurable accomplishment, and to do what I do with heart and soul and full attention, not measuring it against anyone else's productivity, or even against my own past performance. Planning a workshop, speaking with a student, folding the laundry, running an errand, writing my book, or trying to get my singing voice back, I want to take all the time I need to do it well, not begrudge it the attention, care, and love it asks of me.

This is a very different mindset from happily crossing items off a list and feeling good about how much I've achieved that day. But if while accomplishing external tasks we cheat ourselves out of the present moment, what meaning do our lives have? Again Helen Luke expresses this so beautifully, when she writes:

> We hurry through the so-called boring things in order to attend to that which we deem more important and interesting. Perhaps the final freedom will be a recognition that everything in every moment is "essential" and that nothing at all is "important"![20]

Perhaps the etymologies of the words Luke has enclosed in quotation marks shed some light here. "Essential" derives from the Latin *esse* or "to be," while "essence" has the same root as "existence," and "es" refers to that which *"is, exists, is true."* "Important," on the other hand, stems from *importare* or "to bring in," which came during the Middle Ages to mean "to imply" or "mean." Is it too far-fetched to interpret Luke's words as a reminder that there is something bedrock and unshakeable (*essence*) underlying our feeble attempts to assign a hierarchy of significance (*importance*), that we should surrender the hierarchy and simply allow ourselves to *be,* I wonder?

March 3rd

Today I had another thought about our need to be busy. It can keep us from having to face the inner emptiness, the despair Marion Woodman observes among her analysands, over their sense that, when they go home, *there's no one there.* Marion says,

> So many people who have lost their marriage or relationship go to their apartment at night and can scarcely put their key in the lock. They are flooded with loneliness. Darkness is all there is on the other side of that door. They project their own emptiness into the space. There is nobody home. It's a tragic waste of life.[21]

I know people who plan their lives so that they rarely have to spend an evening alone at home. An exhausting round of social engagements, committee meetings, and visits to the gym ensures that when they finally arrive home late at night, there is just enough time to brush their teeth and fall into bed before the alarm clock rings and they begin again. I've done that myself. Especially during my twenties when it felt as if the whole world was out there having a good time, except me. I remember how reluctant I was to stay in alone and cook dinner for myself. No doubt that's the real hunger I was attempting to assuage with my all too frequent pints of Dairyland ice cream. I knew it, even then, but felt powerless to stop myself. Like Woodman's patients, I was trying to fill my inner emptiness.

But, if not by our busy schedules, how *do* we define ourselves to each other? In a society that asks, "What do you do?" as its introductory greeting, is it any wonder that we feel compelled to answer "a hell of a lot"? "I walk, listen to music, meditate, and write in my journal," is hardly an acceptable response. Although those might indeed be the most important dimensions of a person's life during a particular moment in time, they surely don't get anyone prestige or a paycheck. So we dismiss them as "leisure activities" not worth mentioning in circumstances where we need to demonstrate our own importance in the world. But if our definition of who we are is based primarily on what we do from nine to five, five days a week, in order to pay the rent, it has to be an impoverished answer, at best. Even if we enjoy our work, even if we're passionate about it, there's so much more to who we are as creative members of the human family. And all of that defines who we are more than any official job title ever can.

I thought earlier today that one of the things I love about being forty-three and self-employed is that I am free to decide for myself what a productive day looks like. As I page through my journals from the past three or four years, I find the days that have felt most satisfying were days in which I've combined four or five activities and enjoyed all of them.

Often I start the day with a quiet half hour writing in my journal followed by several hours of writing or editing, then head to the gym or out for a walk with Steve. Afterward I might spend an hour or two preparing for class, bake chocolate chip cookies for the workshop, make a telephone call or two, get supper started, and throw a load of laundry into the washer. After dinner, perhaps a little reading or paper grading, and some television, or more time with my journal. By evening, I almost always feel that it was a peaceful, varied, quietly fulfilling day, right and left brain hemispheres both engaged. On such a day, I've usually had no external acclaim, nor felt my work being validated in any significant sense, none of the typical ego reinforcements that carry us through our lives. And yet it's rewarding, rich, and fertile. I often get ideas for workshops, for writing projects, for cakes, quilts, and other sewing projects. My imagination has had time and space to soar. How wonderful if all my days could hold that quiet satisfaction.

March 4th

An article in Sunday's *New York Times* caught my eye: "Sewing: 30 Million Women Can't Be Wrong." The news that home sewing is once again dramatically on the rise is startling; even more so, the claim that one of three American women between the ages of twenty-five and fifty-five sews. And it's not in order to save money, as in the past. According to this article, women today sew primarily for creative enjoyment and relaxation.

Yes. There is something about the process of combining colors and textures with patterns and styles that is satisfying in a tangible and immediate way. Wearing something one has created oneself or seeing someone else wear it is also very gratifying. I still remember how engrossed I became in the details of designing my "gypsy skirts" in the late 1970s—after I returned from five months of gypsying through Europe and the Middle East—in the process of coordinating fabric and laces, ribbons and beadwork. Inspired by the beautiful Slavic dress and embroidery I'd sketched in my journal in the National Yugoslavian Costume Museum, my masterpiece was a beautiful long, flowing black skirt with a wide border of ivory lace, pearls, gold braid, and jewel-colored trims along the bottom edge. I wore it until it fell apart, then patched it up until it was beyond salvaging. As I strolled in downtown Vancouver one day, a stranger approached me and offered me $200 for it, then and there!

But how fascinating that, at a time when clothes have never been more affordable (due, alas, in no small measure to the mass exploitation of Chinese workers), women are picking up needle and thread once again. I think we do all crave some form of hands-on creativity and self-expression, some direct channel of feeling from heart to hands, and sewing offers both aesthetic and practical rewards that make it ideal. In fact, just reading that article made me want to start sewing again.

The trusty Singer sewing machine has, I think, become a symbol of the simple life—practical and holistic, integrated and serene—that so many of us aspire to. And even if frugality isn't the main issue, the fact is that it's usually less expensive to sew a good quality item of clothing than to buy it. Still, I think it's the creative possibilities that appeal most powerfully to women today, torn and fragmented as we often are—the chance to make something useful and beautiful with our own hands. As Anne Morrow Lindbergh put it in 1955,

> Nothing feeds the center so much as creative work, even humble kinds like cooking and sewing. Baking bread, weaving cloth, putting up preserves, teaching and singing to children, must have been far more nourishing than being the family chauffeur or shopping at super-markets, or doing housework with mechanical aids.[22]

I know this is true for me. It explains the moments of deep satisfaction I experience as I bake a cake for the workshop or chop ginger and onions for a huge pot of curry that will take us through a wintery week. The same thing is true of patchwork and all the other sewing I have done over the years. My soul is nourished and my center is fed in the doing.

March 8th

Just the act of copying out a quote from Helen Nearing's *Loving and Leaving the Good Life* has a calming effect on me. Even if I can't live as uncompromising a life as they did, the underlying principles are so inspiring. "Have less, Be more" is how Helen characterized their philosophy of living—what an important lesson for us today!

It encourages me even in our far more modest attempts to cut down on consumption and clear more time and space for worthy pastimes. They never seemed at a loss, finding tremendous satisfaction in building everything themselves, raising more than enough food for their own needs, and being, in general, amazingly self-sufficient. That's more than I aspire to, but I can surely understand their satisfaction. When I'm immersed in a good project, I feel that way too, whether it's preparing a meal, or sewing a robe for Steve. Toward the end, Helen wrote:

> Perhaps there is only one sin—separateness—with the blessedness of love making all whole. I feel that life is such a unity that love which once happened still exists. It is there on the record. Love once felt has its place. . . . Love is the source, love the goal, and love the method of attainment.[23]

What an affirmation of her own life. And what a beautiful way to end her tribute to her beloved deceased husband, Scott, and their fifty years together. Theirs is the most radical and in a sense perhaps the purest vision of simple living I have yet encountered, partly because personal politics and fundamental belief systems were at stake for them. They were absolutely uncompromising in their passion to live out and embody their values—spiritual, social, and aesthetic.

I don't envision us moving to a large woodsy acreage in order to do subsistence farming. We both need a few more creature comforts than that, and Steve is not interested in a hundred and one ways to build our home with his own hands. But the beauty of simple living is that it doesn't have to be all or nothing. There is an infinite variety of gentler modes of simplification possible. Some we already practice; some we are trying to weave into our life (more conscious consumption), and some we still aspire to and hope to realize over time. I think it's probably a never-ending process.

Again awareness seems to be crucial. One's whole life, one's integrity on every level must be involved. As Duane Elgin says in *Voluntary Simplicity*, it's not only our consumption patterns that have to change; interpersonal communication and work must be infused with honesty, authenticity, and directness, if we are really seeking to simplify our lives.

March 16th

Last Friday night I walked in Manhattan in a torrential downpour to meet Barbara for dinner, enjoying the bustle of people heading home after another hectic work week. It reminded me of how I loved living in Bloomsbury, in the center of London. How easy it was to get to Southampton Row, to the post office and the health food store, to University College and the British Library. Just thinking about it fills me with nostalgia.

How complex and contradictory our desires are. One part of me thrives in the heart of things. Step out of the building and you're immediately somewhere. You can go to a concert at a moment's notice, find yourself surrounded by half a dozen fine ethnic restaurants, and never feel isolated, caught up easily in the city's reassuring, anonymous nonstop activity. Another part of me dreams of a quieter, greener existence with a small organic garden, a patio on which to eat breakfast and write, and abundant peace and natural beauty as a setting for our creative work. That's why the Kitsilano and Point Grey neighborhoods in Vancouver have such appeal. With their proximity to English Bay and the university, the many cafés, bookstores, and cinemas, and their quiet, tree-lined avenues, they combine the best of both worlds. I hope we make wise decisions when we move, decisions that give both of us what we need and enable us to share it too. I have always dreamed of creating a home that would serve as an oasis of comfort for others as well as ourselves. Soon we will have that opportunity.

March 17th

Steve and I discussed simplicity on our walk today. He feels that the complexity and fragmentation we all feel in our lives are the direct result of our loss of connectedness with one another. I'm sure he is right. People searching for a simpler life are often also searching for community. I know that I yearn for more of both.

Because we don't have intact relationships anymore and feel ourselves isolated, surrounded by strangers, we are often on the defensive, knowing we have to protect ourselves and our own interests. Things don't flow smoothly or easily. We don't step in for each other as far as caretaking is concerned. Families with children are often on their own and must arrange childcare themselves. Most often there are no doting grandparents or other relatives nearby to step in and ease the burden.

The medical and legal fields reflect this fragmentation also. Gone is the lifelong family doctor who really cares about the patient, and lawyers for their part appear far more concerned with winning cases and making fat profits than with justice or finding out the truth. I won't even start on the corporate world.

March 23rd

We picked up our first shipment of organic produce from the Purple Dragon Co-op yesterday; it was a beautifully colorful assortment of apples, tiny green bananas, tangellos, pears, grapefruits, broccoli, cauliflower, carrots, parsnips, green peppers, tomatoes, celery, leeks, spinach, Romaine lettuce, zucchini, and eggplant. Perhaps this wealth of organic fruits and vegetables will get us eating more healthfully, because I'm bound and determined that the time has come.

March 30th

Tonight I shall simply allow myself to feel downhearted, without trying to deny or talk myself out of it. I feel discouraged and perhaps even a little overlooked, and so I will stay "close to the zero" line and just quietly and slowly work away. Maybe I'll feel better tomorrow. Meanwhile, stay engaged and productive, as much as possible.

April 4th

Not only does simplicity mean something different for every person, it remains an ever-changing process for each of us. Perhaps there will never be a time when we know we have arrived. It will simply become more and more our natural mode of thinking and feeling, indeed, a way of life. Perhaps the false alternatives will gradually drop away, like clothes we have outgrown, or tired emotions that dissipate with time, and Anne Morrow Lindbergh's "singleness of eye" and "purity of intention" will emerge. And maybe it's a matter of seeing more and more clearly what has been there all along, how we can bring our lives into harmony with our soul's deepest yearnings. Because those cannot be measured or quantified—and will never be satisfied by material luxury.

April 7th

Yesterday I offered my one-day intensive workshop on "Journal Writing and the Art of Simple Living." Eight women, ranging in age from thirty to sixty, wrote together and shared ideas about everything from clearing out clutter and renewing the commitment to our own physical well-being to coping with involuntary downscaling. What kept coming up time and time again were references to "stuff," that amorphous term for undifferentiated, opaque substance that clogs our lives with its presence like dregs of food caught in the kitchen sink, or worse yet, like arterial plaque in our veins. Karen described how her involuntary retirement as a high-profile radio talk-show host prompted a process of soul-searching that led her to a whole new career path, which now includes conducting her own journal workshops. I shared my experience of considering a professional position last year and being very clear that it was not what I wanted, although the prestige and salary were tempting. Ellen said that having so much free time was a mixed blessing, but she didn't go into detail. I think she was referring to the pressure she puts on herself to use that time productively. The importance of community and connectedness came up over and over again.

In keeping with the day's theme, I offered a relatively simple lunch. I'd made a large dish of broccoli and cheese pie, and set out various breads from Zabar's, a large platter with Brie, grapes, and honeydew melon, and homemade chocolate squares and poppyseed cake for dessert. In the morning as they arrived there was a plate of banana-pecan and hazelnut-fig breads for those who hadn't taken time for breakfast.

It was a serene and peaceful day of writing in community. Jarda rang this morning to say she had experienced a wonderful sense of shared purpose, harmony, and trust. Perhaps there was something "especially special" about this workshop. I don't know; I feel that way about each one. Now I'm looking forward to the six-week workshop series that starts on Wednesday night. And I'm feeling, once again, how fortunate I am that the various dimensions of my work flow together so organically, making it easy for me to pursue what is most important to me.

Today: a little writing, grading, exercise, cooking, and some time to relax and unwind after yesterday's purposeful activity.

Hazelnut Fig Bread (two loaves)

1 cup hazelnuts, roasted and ground*
3 cups unbleached flour (can substitute up to half whole
   wheat flour)
1 cup oat bran
2 T. baking powder
1/2 tsp. salt
8 ounces dried figs (remove stems and soak figs in
   enough water to cover them for several hours or
   overnight, then drain)
2 cups milk or soymilk
4 eggs
1 cup brown sugar
1/2 cup melted butter or canola oil

* Put hazelnuts in a baking dish in a preheated 350 degree
oven for 10 minutes. Rub off skins, and when cool, grind in
blender.

Mix flour, oat bran, baking powder, salt, and ground
hazelnuts in a large bowl. In blender, purée figs with milk,
eggs, brown sugar, and butter or oil. Pour liquid mixture
over dry ingredients and mix just until they are combined.
Pour batter into two loaf pans that have been greased or
sprayed with Pam. Bake 40–45 minutes at 350-375 degrees.
Leave loaves in pans for an hour to cool off. This is very
good with butter, or cream cheese or other mild cheeses.

April 9th

I am thinking of telling our department chairman that I'm available to teach an additional course this fall, so that I can contribute
more to my newly established tax-deferred annuity. Assuming that
works out, how can I arrange my schedule so I still have time to
write?

I could increase bulk-cooking and freeze some casseroles. Eat a lot of raw salads and let Steve prepare some of them. Do laundry at night when I'm too tired to do anything else, instead of during the day, as a means of procrastinating. Cut down on gym visits to save travel time. Possibly overlap some course readings and assignments where appropriate, between my "Modern Culture" and "Women and Literature" classes, for example. Use short time intervals to clean and organize.

Prepare in bulk: meat sauce, chicken cacciatore, lasagna, curry, banana and pumpkin breads, and corn muffins. As long as we belong to the organic produce co-op, I'll always keep making soups. We don't seem to tire of them. Mum makes soup of whatever she has in the garden, refrigerator, or freezer, often throwing in leftovers from an earlier meal. Even when her combinations seem haphazard to me, there's no denying that the results are always delicious and unexpected, no two pots the same. *"Man nehme was man hat,"* she says, quoting an old German proverb. Use whatever is available.

If I prepare a semester's worth of food before the term begins, it won't be too bad, even with three courses and my usual workshop series. But I will have to be ruthless about getting to my study by eight o'clock each morning, come what may, and holding that time sacrosanct. No appointments, telephone calls, or other distractions. Every term I envision how productive I would like to be, but all too often I take the path of least resistance, welcoming all kinds of diversions from the work I've planned.

Meanwhile, here are my general directions for a tasty cacciatore.

Chicken Cacciatore (for four)

3–4 pounds of chicken pieces, skinned (you can use whatever is on sale that week)
2–3 medium onions, chopped
2 garlic cloves, chopped (or as much as you like)
1 tsp. each of dried oregano and basil

fresh parsley and chives, if available
a large can of crushed tomatoes (or a jar of prepared
    tomato sauce)
1–2 pounds of chopped vegetables, any combination of
    peppers, zucchini, mushrooms, leeks, broccoli, car-
    rots, celery
salt and pepper to taste

Put skinned chicken pieces in a roaster or large casserole. (If time permits, brown them in a frying pan in a little olive oil first.) Put chopped onions and garlic on top, then add other vegetables and sprinkle oregano and basil over mixture. Pour crushed tomatoes over top and add salt and pepper to taste. (You can also add a teaspoon of sugar for a milder taste.) Bake covered at 375 degrees for approximately an hour or until chicken slips easily off bones. Check halfway, stir thoroughly with a wooden spoon, and add a little water or red wine if it isn't almost covered with liquid. You can add black olives and/or capers a few minutes before serving. Serve over pasta and sprinkle generously with Parmesan cheese. I always double or triple the recipe and freeze most of it in small casserole dishes. If I plan to serve it to company, I use boneless chicken whenever possible.

April 18th

Again I have been noticing how often the word "stuff" comes up in my Wednesday night writing circle. Everyone seems to be trying to clear theirs out. Many in the group feel oppressed by their material possessions and overwhelmed by the thought of having to sort out what they need and want from what should be given away or thrown out. The word itself is onomatopoeic. "Stuff" sounds opaque, heavy, and burdensome, and suggests precisely the clogging effect it does in fact have.

Women tell of attics jammed full of items they know they'll never use again but can't seem to throw out. We laugh at our common foibles. What are we trying to hold on to by keeping things we haven't even looked at for twenty or thirty years? Tangible proof that we were once young? Objects that hint at the story of our lives? Echoes of relationships long past? Once again Marion Woodman says it so well:

> One of the wonderful results of my own aging has been that my life has become a lot simpler. What is superfluous has been stripped away. It is such a relief to see it go. It takes a lot of work to simplify. It takes what I would call a very good sense of the inner masculine to discern what needs to stay and what needs to go. . . . Simplifying is crucial. If we are still trying to figure out how to care for our too large house and garden, and what to do with all our goods and chattels, we can't let go into a new life.[24]

Yes, it does require considerable discernment to determine what goes and what stays. And maybe this stripping away of what is superfluous is a gradual process. The longer we stay with the process and begin to feel its liberating effects, the more we can bear to part with, aware that lightening our material load releases energy for other things.

What is the new life I want to "let go into"?

April 19th

When she was asked how she managed to write books while raising her sons as a single parent, Toni Morrison offered a valuable insight into the simplifying process. She said that she'd made a list of everything she *had* to do, large and small, then a second list of everything she *wanted* to do. In the process she discovered, "There were only two things without which I couldn't live: mother my children and write books. Then I cut out everything that didn't have to do with those two things."[25]

Talk about an efficient if ruthless method of streamlining. "There was an urgency—that's all I remember," she says. There must have been a great deal she sacrificed, but she accomplished what she desired most because she was absolutely clear about what that was. And she was prepared to pay the price, to let go of everything else in order to have time for it. What do I value most?

What do I *have* to do? Live as a conscious and decent human being. Be a loving and considerate wife, daughter, sister, friend, and a responsible college teacher. Be financially responsible. Assume legal responsibility for my schizophrenic brother some day. Not necessarily in this order of importance.

What do I *want* to do? All of the above. Write books. Have a child. Sing. Spend more time with friends. Spend more time outdoors. Laugh a lot. Read. Exercise. Run. Dance. Sew. Travel to India, South America, and back to Europe. Study Jung in more depth. Take care of my health. Move back to Vancouver. Work with women and journal writing. Create beauty around me.

What are the things without which I could not live? Steve. Our cherishing love for each other. My journal. Books. Loving human bonds. Nature. Beauty. The feeling that I have something to give to others. Music. Movement and exercise. The ocean and the mountains.

Toni Morrison had it down to two things. For me those would be Steve and writing. But how grateful I am for all the others as well.

What a wonderful journal writing topic this is.

April 20th

Is it less of the life we already have that we think of when we think of simple living? Or is it something else altogether? Not just a quantitative change, but a wholly different mode of being in the world?

April 21st

"Clarity" is another word that keeps coming up in the group. It's absolutely fundamental to the simplifying process. Because simple living is more than a collection of acquired techniques; it's a coherent way of understanding one's place and purpose in the world.

Even if you start by deciding to cut back several external commitments a week, for example, that's not all there is to simplifying. There is the reflective process. What do I cut out, and why? Where does that "found" time go? The same questions can be asked in relation to any attempt to simplify. Whatever the original intention may be, starting the process will set other processes in motion as well. It won't stay contained as a single action, deed, or idea.

Perhaps the spiritual dimension of simplicity is related to being "pure of heart," guileless, frank and transparent, with nothing to hide. Once again, this seems to require tremendous vigilance, consciousness, self-understanding. Because we're not children, after all. As intelligent and experienced adults, we know of the many alternatives available to us, and we cannot go back to the Garden of Eden, where choice was not a burden. To pretend otherwise would simply be bad faith. I'm beginning to sense that the possibilities for self-deception in relation to simple living, as elsewhere, are endless.

April 22nd

Several years ago I ended my membership in the Modern Languages Association. I had never been active in their various activities, and the monthly publication, full of abstruse, rarified literary theory was taking over my study. I offered it to our college library, but they already had it and so, with the sadness characteristic of the true bibliophile, I reluctantly bundled up five years' worth of issues and put them out for recycling.

A year later I bowed out of the National Women's Studies Association as well. Not without uneasiness, because women's organizations frequently struggle to stay alive, but I did finally follow my inclination to at least take a break and think the matter of membership through. The amount of printed matter that arrived in the mail, mostly concerning conferences across the country that I could not attend, seemed wasteful.

Since *A Voice of Her Own* was published, I've received invitations to join various groups and organizations, but the only one I have taken up so far is the National Journal Network, a small grassroots movement of passionate journal writers. This brings the total of my memberships to three (including the International Women's Writing Guild and the Staten Island Coalition for the Arts and Humanities). The amount of related paper is manageable, and I usually find time to read most of what they send me. Besides personal enrichment, I have nothing to gain or lose through these memberships, so there's no need to subscribe for strategic purposes. It's not that I think organizations are a bad idea, or that people shouldn't belong to them. But I think the temptation to do so indiscriminately and unthinkingly, as if membership will automatically enhance professional status, is very powerful and, like anything else, can have an addictive edge.

It may be that for those on more conventional career tracks, professional memberships are an important tool for that activity that irritates me more than anything: networking. I can't help but interpret this as "looking for influential people who can help me rise up the ladder of success." My friends who live in that world tell me it doesn't have to be that sordid, but the thought of sizing people up for their potential usefulness chills my soul.

Perhaps, too, I suspect that nonstop professional activity can become a means of avoiding one's own inner life, just as working long hours of voluntary overtime, according to a recent article in *The New York Times*, has become a means of avoiding tensions at home. (Apparently the workplace has become "home" to many Americans, while dealing with dirty dishes, needy kids, and messy emotions "has become work.") Endless meetings can serve as one more item on the already overloaded list that demonstrates our importance, indeed, indispensability, to the world around us.

I know people who thrive on racing from one emergency board meeting to the next. Yet when I try to engage them in conversation, I get the sense that there's no one there. Ask them the most basic question involving even a modicum of self-reflectiveness, and their eyes open wide: "I don't know; I've never thought about that." I don't mean to suggest that only shallow and boring people join organizations. Of course I know that in the age of slashed social service budgets and volunteerism, many wonderful groups of all kinds do great good that wouldn't get done otherwise.

Perhaps membership in groups is not incompatible with simple living when the group's aims are in line with our own deepest sense of what is necessary and valuable in society. I suppose it's thoughtful and selective membership I believe in, not just unthinkingly paying the dues of the relevant professional association. If I knew I had only two or three years left to live, would I still do it? Not that we can always live with the thought of our own inevitable demise before our eyes, but on an occasional basis, it's not a bad barometer of what holds authentic value. And, of course, like everything else, these are reflections in process. Next year, next month, I could decide to rejoin the NWSA.

April 23rd

Pamela, in the Wednesday night workshop, has just been diagnosed with breast cancer. I put myself uneasily in her position, and feel the terrifying threat of losing everything precious to me, including the possibility of my own future.

Last night I browsed in a book Steve just picked up, entitled *The Absent Body,* and read, "Being ill is before all alienation from the world." I found myself thinking about how lonely and isolated Mum has felt throughout the many years of chronic illness and disease, and about her need to talk about her symptoms. The author, Drew Leder, explains the sick person's sense of alienation in moving terms.

> The natural expression of compassion is service. . . . One-body compassion for my sick friend leads me to do what I can for her: hold her hand, offer words of comfort, bring her food, fix her bedclothes. I give over my motoric possibilities to be guided by her desires. If she is thirsty, my hands fetch her drink. If she is weak, my limbs supply her strength. We act as if we were one functioning body. . . . It is this embracing of relation as much as the specific actions I perform, that brings about the relief of suffering. For her suffering is based partially in the experience of isolation . . . pain and disease disrupt communion with the natural and social world, creating a lived solipsism. When another consents to form one body even with the ill body—one in pain, contorted, or disabled—this exerts a healing force. The isolation imposed by illness is somewhat overcome.[26]

What a beautiful description of the healing power of empathy. This is what we all want to do for Pamela. It's what I yearn to offer my mother, who has, I know, felt so alone with her chronic pain over the years. Whether or not we are physically together, I want to join forces with her, offer her my own health and strength as a support for her body so she doesn't feel so isolated in her suffering.

Leder's idea of "one-body compassion" accounts for the power of healing practices such as therapeutic touch and shiatsu as well, it seems to me. When the practitioner places her bodily strength and focused attention at the service of her patient, a transfer of health, energy, and love can occur and this helps to mobilize the patient's own healing instincts. And this brings me back to a beautiful passage near the end of *Lost in Translation,* where Eva Hoffman reflects,

> It is only in the knowledge of our own ephemerality and the passage of time that things gain their true dimension, and we begin to feel the simplicity of being alive. It is only that knowledge that is large enough to cradle a tenderness for everything that is always to be lost—a tenderness for each of our moments, for others and for the world.[27]

The "simplicity of being alive" is, I think, the assurance that we are resting in life, moment by moment, and seeing through superficial appearances to the vulnerability and fragility of everything that lives. That we are seeing what is really there, in other words, and loving it, just as it is. Dropping roles and masks, lofty pretences and false appearances, we live from a deep inner conviction. This is part of it, I am sure.

April 25th

In *Plain and Simple: A Woman's Journey to the Amish,* Sue Bender has a wonderful discussion of the addictive quality of lists. She writes,

> A tyranny of lists engulfed me. The lists created the illusion that my life was full [but] I never thought to stop and ask myself, "What really matters?" Instead, I gave everything equal weight. I had no way to select what

> was important and what was not. . . . By evening, the list
> had become a battlefield of hieroglyphics, crossed-off
> areas, checks and circles . . . to remind me of all the tasks
> that didn't get done. Tomorrow's list began with today's
> leftovers. I never questioned my frantic behavior.[28]

I understand how making lists can become a trap, even an addiction, as she claims it was for her. But it hasn't worked that way for me. Given the absence of external structure in my professional life, the process of jotting down a list of the day's activities—often as part of my morning journal entry—helps me get an overall sense of how the day might shape up. As I feel my way through it, usually there's an instinctive sense of what is most important—not according to any absolute scale of significance, but *for me on this particular day*. It might be reading a batch of student essays, or having a lengthy writing session, or getting some pressing errands out of the way so that I have clear mental space inside me.

Once I have things down on paper, I no longer have the nagging sense that I could be forgetting something important. As I move fluidly through the day and check things off, I do experience a small sense of accomplishment. Particularly on days when I'm feeling unmotivated and adrift, my list reassures me that I'm actually getting something done. Often there are a few things left undone at the end of the day, but that doesn't bother me. I know from experience that I'm overly optimistic about how much I can do, so I simply carry them over to the next day and begin again.

April 28th

How can I open my heart so that more love and goodwill can flow in and out? This is what I want more than anything, yet I seem to struggle so much. No wonder Elisabeth Kübler-Ross says at the end of her autobiography that "the hardest lesson to learn is unconditional love."[29] At this moment, it doesn't feel like a simple task. I feel isolated. I yearn for passionate friendship. There seem to be too many barriers everywhere. I feel judgmental and critical, perhaps because that need is unmet—or is it the other way around? I feel unappreciated at the College. Too often, I feel starved for beauty, emotionally blocked and bodily inhibited, and drained by Steve's intermittent depression.

And I feel defensive about this book. My old demons haunt me: "Why waste your time, you're not saying anything profound or original anyway." I feel lethargic, unmotivated, uninspired, and blocked by what I deem my too expansive and academic style of writing. Today I feel nothing but self-criticism, especially where my writing is concerned.

April 29th

It's exactly six months today since I embarked on this year of simple living. Halfway through my second journal of exploration, what have I discovered along the way?

First—there's nothing particularly *easy* about simple living. And it does not mean merely doing less of what we have been doing all along.

Second—it involves a whole new way of being conscious in day-to-day life. It's an ongoing and changing process of expanding awareness. What doesn't change is the need to stay alert, to strive for clarity and understanding at many levels.

Third—there is no objective standard by which simplicity can be measured. It's highly individual and there are no hard and fast signs informing us that we have arrived. Rather, it's a process of peeling away successive layers of accumulated clutter, emotional as well as material, just like the proverbial onion.

Fourth—it's related to our core life issues and values. How we live comes down to what we believe, who we think we are, and what we care about most deeply.

Fifth—it involves paying careful attention to one thing at a time, to whatever we are doing at the moment.

On a practical level, I have found that simple living involves feeling close to nature, communicating as honestly as I can and living with integrity, getting rid of outdated clutter—things, causes, activities—that no longer hold meaning for me, owning and maintaining only what I need, keeping financial matters as straightforward as possible and being very clear about what my money is for, and eating healthfully and getting some kind of exercise every day.

Let's see what the next six months bring.

May 1st

At last I am losing weight again. Perhaps this weight loss will turn out to be like the big one I experienced twenty years ago, when I lost seventy-five pounds. Then, too, it took place in two major stages. I lost more than half of it, stabilized over a period of a year, then dropped the remaining thirty pounds in a fairly short period of time. This time I'm following a similar pattern; the second stage began about a month ago. Perhaps my body has needed that time to reorient itself. However, the weight is coming off more grudgingly this time. I've read that this is to be expected after the age of forty. Even so, I lost close to fifty pounds in six months in 1995, and that included three weeks of travel and good food in Europe.

I'm doing it in a healthier fashion this time around. In my early twenties, I thought of all calories as being equal. Of course I knew that ice cream and cinnamon buns lacked any nutrients whatsoever, but I "spent" my 800 or 1000 calories a day largely on comfort food, which was too often junk food. No wonder I could peel off my fingernails like layers of an onion. This time around I'm more concerned with eating wisely and paying attention to what my body needs, including exercise. Since May 1995 I have worked out at the gym three times a week and walked on average an hour a day.

Whenever I have achieved a significant weight loss over the years, it has always been in relation to sustained and consistent exercise, whether aerobic classes, jogging, or simply, as in 1977, tremendous amounts of walking.

Diets have never worked for me. My first visit to a Weight Watchers meeting ended with a stop at the Dairy Queen on the way home, in anticipation of all the deprivation I'd be feeling in the months to follow. I refuse to buy all kinds of diet foods and formulas. I'm eating real food now, but trying to become more finely attuned to what my body really wants. Babies eat only what they want, I'm told, and they seem instinctively to choose a healthy balance of nutrients. As adults we lose touch with our natural bodily appetites and overlay them with "shoulds" and "oughts," just as we do with everything else in our lives. I'm trying to tune in again.

But, much as I may want to, I can't create the readiness to do this, to actually listen to my body. It's so much easier just to eat thoughtlessly, out of habit, for comfort and consolation when I'm feeling bored, depressed, or weary. To counter a lifetime of ingrained faulty eating habits takes constant attentiveness. Conscious eating is, for me, the only way to lose weight in a healthy way. I have to ask myself: Is this what I need in order to have energy and health? Do I need to eat more, or am I satisfied? Will a mouthful or two of chocolate (or ice cream or cheesecake) be a pleasant ending to dinner, or will it set off my sweet tooth, and lead to excess? Is it all right to go to bed feeling empty, or shall I eat a small snack?

It's the most intelligent weight loss method of all, but it's not a quick fix, nor can it be effectively packaged and sold. And it won't make anybody rich. Conscious eating is very difficult for anyone with a food addiction, but it's so powerful. And so simple. In the old days, any circumstance out of the ordinary presented a problem. Because diets invite an attitude of "all or nothing," I felt at risk of blowing my diet and agonized in advance about what to do. Our trip to Washington, D.C., last week, for example, would have presented many eating dangers, especially our dinners out. I'd have "blown" the diet and probably stuffed down dessert, just because I knew that when the trip was over, I'd be forcing myself back onto the diet. In fact, it wasn't like that at all. We ate dinner in Indian and Moroccan restaurants, and I ordered exactly what I wanted, both times. I didn't stuff myself and I didn't order dessert. I just had a bite of Steve's. No problem.

So why is something this obvious and straightforward so difficult to remember? Who could have convinced me, twenty years ago, that losing weight has nothing to do with diets, fat free and sugarless products (or even prescription drugs, which I never did try), but could be achieved through just a few simple steps? Pay careful attention to what you eat, and eat only what your body wants. Get your body moving and exercise more. Get enough sleep so you don't eat out of fatigue. Keep a journal and pour your heart out freely.

It really is that simple. What isn't so simple is to predict the timing. For months and years I "will" myself to change my eating habits and nothing works. Then one day, effortlessly, something clicks and I'm on the way. Suddenly I experience symptoms of what can only be described as a normal relationship with food. It is one of life's sensual pleasures, but not a source of emotional comfort. I want to move more, and I feel more intimately at home in my body. I feel more sexual. I have more energy, feel lighter and more buoyant. It feels like a state of grace.

And it all begins with an elusive, undefinable shift in consciousness. It has nothing to do with self-denial or deprivation, rules or restrictions. The guidance is internal and comes, gently, from the part of me that wants "to have life and to have it more abundantly"; that yearns for spirit to illuminate matter; that longs for energy, gracefulness, and vitality in my body, and hungers for music, dance, and beauty in my life.

There is something shockingly simple in all of this, in eating exactly what our bodies crave, and just the right amount to satisfy ourselves. Perhaps, with care and attention over time, I can turn this state of grace into my normal way of being in the world. I suppose it comes down to listening to our bodies, something we manage so effectively *not* to do most of the time. What intrigues me is that we have become so alienated that we trust the diet experts to tell us what our bodies really know all along, and what no one else can know for us.

May 2nd

After last night's wild thunderstorm and the howling winds that woke me up at 4 a.m., it is very still now, hyper-clear and brilliant this morning. Soon I'll head out for a walk. A beautiful, open day stretches out before me. My women's book group meets tonight, so I have an excuse to reread Charlotte Perkins Gilman's "The Yellow Wallpaper" and Doris Lessing's "To Room Nineteen."

This whole week I've felt so grateful for the time I have available. Not that I've made particularly good use of it, but every day, as I've headed out for the midday walk my body has been craving, I am so thankful that I can do this, and guiltily aware that most people only dream of having this kind of freedom. Twice this week Steve and I walked on the boardwalk in radiant sunshine at a time of day when most people are on their fifteen-minute afternoon coffee break, assuming they are fortunate enough to have one. The handful of other walkers we encountered were either young mothers with children in strollers, or retired couples. Luxury. One of the greatest pleasures of our quiet life together, those afternoon and early evening walks by the ocean, a shared delight and passion.

I have been thinking that a semester without any problem students is such a fine experience. It takes the stress out of teaching when I'm not forced to squander energy dealing with immature and inappropriate classroom behavior. After last semester's nasty episode with Mary Ann, a psychotic older student whose behavior I am not trained to handle, I've been holding my breath, but it has turned out to be a peaceful and satisfying term. I hope summer session will follow suit.

Yesterday I had an interesting conversation with a student I had not met before. Lisa came to my office asking if I would supervise an independent study project over the summer so that she could graduate with a bachelor of arts degree in August. I was surprised when she told me our graduate supervisor had given her my name, since he surely knows adjuncts are not paid for anything other than lecture time, not even for weekly office hours which many of us nevertheless hold. I explained to Lisa that I could not, as a matter of principle, take on any more unpaid work as an adjunct faculty member. She seemed to take it as a personal affront and left in a hurry, leaving me to wonder if I'd come across as selfish and money-grubbing. I was also rather annoyed with our graduate supervisor for putting me in such an awkward position.

I don't feel bitter about my adjunct status. I'm there by choice, and it works out well for me in many ways. But along with the realization that I will never be offered a tenure-track position at the College of Staten Island has come the freedom not to curry favor in hopes of future rewards. And I simply won't contribute to the growing institutionalization of adjunct labor, wherein part-time faculty with abysmal pay and no job security or benefits are asked to take on more and more responsibilities for which we receive neither remuneration nor recognition. In the past academic year I have been asked—illegally, it turns out—to attend program meetings on days on which I don't teach, to serve as a faculty mentor to the annual Women's Studies publication, and to supervise independent study work. All without pay, of course. What really riled me in the case above was that the student said she'd already approached one full-time faculty member who refused, saying that since he wouldn't receive extra pay, he wouldn't do it. What does he think he is being paid his cushy salary for? He earns at least four times what I do and supervising independent studies is part of his job description.

I teach to the best of my ability. I call troubled students at home and violate union regulations by holding unpaid office hours, because I refuse to penalize students for the City University's short-sightedness in refusing to pay adjuncts a living wage. But I will not take on any more responsibilities of full-time faculty—only a few of whom, ironically, have my academic background or publication record—at one quarter of their salary. That would set a dangerous precedent and I will have no part of it.

May 3rd

It is heavy, gray, and wet out today. I woke up late to the relentless pounding of wind and rain against the bedroom window and knew at once it would be a low-key "internal" day of quiet activity, in contrast to the past week of high energy, sunshine-inspired comings and goings. Each year when the balmy air and May lilacs arrive, spring fever hits me every bit as fiercely as it did twenty years ago and I find myself inventing errands in order to be outside in the sunshine. It's embarrassing. Today I'm content to be inside. I am going to sort through our box of organic produce this afternoon and prepare several meals for the coming week.

May 4th

How abruptly the thickness of meaning can flip over into emptiness and ennui. One moment all is well; the next, I feel a creeping, invidious restlessness and lethargy envelop me. The freedom of my unstructured day begins to feel like a heavy responsibility, and I want an external authority to tell me what needs doing, so I can feel I'm accomplishing something. Sometimes that feeling is fleeting and dissipates as I sit down to work. At other times it feels like depression, brief but real. Then I just have to ride it out. I try to be gentle with myself, think before I open my mouth, and not act out toward Steve or anyone else who happens to cross my path.

Often, doing something, almost anything, can break the evil spell. Sometimes straightening out a room or baking banana bread can dissipate the negative energy. I remember reading that Natalie Goldberg's Zen master told her to "make positive action for the good"[30] when she felt despair. Occasionally, speaking with a friend can alter my internal chemistry, although I often hesitate to call for fear of infecting them with my mood.

The good thing at this point in my life is that I know it won't last. I'm never down for long these days, it seems. The joy of life always seems to pull me back into its orbit and I feel myself once again part of the human race. Present. Alive. Engaged. Now—out for a walk.

May 5th

If simplicity in communication involves speaking frankly and not wasting words, we have to be discriminating and sensitive about what can be said with kindness, since not everything that *can* be said, *should* be said. I'm not always so clear about when I'm speaking frankly with honest intentions, and when I'm merely venting frustration in the course of my so-called honesty. And I'm quite skeptical about people who claim to be perfectly in touch with their own deepest motivations and impulses. Claiming it is much easier than doing it.

Perhaps the key is to observe oneself and to become more aware of the twists and turns of our ego's wish to hold court in the course of conversation. Where appropriate, we might try to share this with each other in the self-reflective mode of dialogue, as it's practiced in Steve's Dialogue and Lifwynn social self-inquiry groups. Perhaps this might open the door to a new level of authenticity in conversation, and to a different kind of intimacy among people.

Now, on to more concrete concerns. I baked two dozen hazelnut-fig muffins this afternoon. I do a great deal of baking when my work-shop is in progress, but baking muffins is somehow different. They symbolize so much to me. Friendship, for one thing; how many times during my university years did I meet Kathie, Laël, or Maureen for coffee and muffin breaks? And community. In London, at Willy G., I baked muffins every weekend and brought them to various friends' rooms for their Sunday morning breakfasts. Comfort and nurtu-rance; sweet, round wholesomeness. And endless variation. During my months of therapy in 1982 I would stop across the street at the Muffin Break every Thursday morning after my session with Michael and sample one of their forty-plus varieties until I decided on peanut butter chocolate chip as my favorite. Decadent and not especially nutritious, but oh, so comforting.

This isn't just my personal symbolism either. Marion Woodman relates a poignant experience with an analysand who'd stopped on the way to her analytic hour to pick up a muffin for Marion, then anguished about whether or not to give it to her. "I don't know about muffins in the States," Woodman says, "but muffins in Canada are numinous...I broke the muffin in two and gave her half. Because of the love that was in the muffin, and because she had been received, it was a communion."[31] The story is about much more than muffins, of course; it's about the giving and receiving of love, and especially about the hunger *to be received*. But I think her patient's symbolic associations to muffins must have been similar to mine.

Synchronistically, the day I related this lovely story to my Journal class at the International Women's Writing Guild Conference last August, a young woman came to me after class, incredulous, and told me that she had picked up some muffins on her way to class that morning, intending to give one to me, and then talked herself out of it, deciding that it was a foolish idea. How fearful we are of having our gifts of love rejected, our loving gestures rebuffed.

Cake is generic; a muffin is personal! Here is one of my favorite recipes.

Blueberry Corn Muffins (one dozen)

1/2 cup softened butter or vegetable oil
1 cup sugar
2 large eggs
1 tsp. vanilla
2 tsp. baking powder
dash of salt
1 1/3 cups unbleached flour (you can substitute whole
    wheat for some or all of it)
2/3 cup cornmeal
1/2 cup milk
2 cups blueberries, fresh or frozen
1 to 2 T. sugar mixed with a sprinkle of cinnamon or
    nutmeg

Heat oven to 375°F. Line a muffin pan with foil or paper cups. In a large bowl, beat butter with sugar until fluffy, then beat in eggs, vanilla, baking powder, and salt. Measure flour and cornmeal together and add to the butter mixture. Fold in milk and blueberries just until mixed. Put batter into muffin cups and sprinkle with cinnamon sugar. Bake for 20–25 minutes until golden on top, and let cool for 15 minutes before taking out of pan. These freeze well and I always double the recipe.

May 6th

This morning I have no clear sense of how the day might unfold. Robbed of immediate purpose—all but two of my students chose the late paper option so now I have no essays to grade—I'm wondering how best to spend my time today.

Spending time. Investing time, saving time, borrowing time, beating time, hoarding time, defying time, managing time, needing time, lacking time, squandering time, buying time, wasting time, gaining time, passing time, using time, taking time, killing time, running out of time, being out of time.

So many metaphors of time. So many ways we construct it. As if it's one more finite and measurable commodity, at our disposal to be wisely invested for maximum return. As if we can manipulate it. Strategize, in order to have more of it, somehow trick the universe into giving us a few extra hours.

How utterly ambivalent we are about time. It is at once our most precious asset and our worst enemy. Obsessed with productivity and generous returns on our investments, we want to control time, stretch and expand it, squeeze every bit of tangible benefit from it. And yet, tragically, in the process we rob ourselves of the present, which is the only time we ever really have.

How telling that new computers are sold with the promise of a response time milliseconds faster and printers promoted as producing six pages per minute instead of three. What is it we think we gain by saving five minutes on a thirty-page print job?

Mediterranean cultures, I imagine, may still experience time differently. Many years ago I stood in a bank line in Italy for half an hour and watched people eat their lunch as they waited. They did not seem to be upset over a delay that would have had most of us speed-driven North Americans apoplectic with frustration. And what about the Southern European habit of stopping after work for a cappuccino with friends or the three-hour, six-course meal that becomes the social focus of the day?

Not long ago I read an article in the *Utne Reader* about "slow food," a Mediterranean movement of counter-resistance to the American fast-food trend of the 1980s. Our North American ambivalence about time is indeed echoed in our attitude toward food. The very concept of "fast food" says it all: the most extravagant excesses of consumption accompanied by our dangerous obsession with slenderness. Societal schizophrenia.

But productivity does not equal meaning. To what end, all of our streamlining and saving of minutes and hours, if we lack a basic conviction of the purpose and meaning of our lives? There's such a painful irony here. We streamline the activities of the day for greatest efficiency, getting rid of the small human exchanges that give our lives warmth and texture. Then we rush off at night to a course on mindfulness or a workshop on walking meditation or building relationships, desperate to reclaim—for a hefty fee—what we have devalued and thrown away.

What if our language reflected a whole other range of metaphors concerned with time? Taking time, savoring time, dwelling in time, loving time, occupying time, cherishing time, honoring time, filling time, flowing with time, bestowing time, lavishing time. Living in these terms would imply an acceptance of time's immanence, a whole different experience from what we are accustomed to. But oh, what peace not to be constantly doing battle with it, trying to overcome time, to beat time back.

What, then, is time for? I have often railed against friends whose work lives take such priority that a simple meal together must be projected five or six weeks into the future, but I know that I, too, am afflicted with the virus of productivity. In freelance creative work the need to feel something has been accomplished at the end of the day seems especially urgent. It becomes a way of vindicating one's decision not to follow "nine to five," and of justifying the hubris required to follow one's creative calling with no promise of eventual success, or even of making a living. In our goal-oriented society it is very difficult to give our creative work all the time it needs. Stephen Nachmanovitch describes this dilemma so well in *Free Play,* my favorite book on the creative process. In one of the passages I taped above my desk while writing *A Voice of Her Own,* he says,

> If I act out of a separation of subject and object—*I,* the subject, working on *it,* the object—then my work is something other than myself; I will want to finish it quickly and get on with my life. . . . But if art and life are one, we feel free to work through each sentence, each note, each color, as though we had infinite amounts of time and energy.[32]

Indeed. Surely, as I know in my heart of hearts, this generous free-flowing bestowal of love and attention is the only way to work. *This* is what time is for. But somebody has got to pay the rent!

May 10th

A spirited discussion was sparked last night in the book group by Gloria's observation that May Sarton's work has been receiving a great deal of bad press lately. I think the telling fact is that Margot Peters' biography was authorized by Sarton herself, so there is no reason to assume it's just Sarton's critics out to nail her.

I do agree that there is something disturbing about the extent to which she seems to have misrepresented herself and her life in her journals written for publication. A journal is defined by honest and truthful writing about oneself, even when it is written for publication. The pact between reader and writer is that the writer has offered the truth as best she could about her life. Perhaps a partial truth, perhaps not including everything that could be said, but certainly not a deliberate distortion or lie. Once the writer actually passes lies off as the truth, she is writing fiction and should either write a fictional journal or at least add a disclaimer at the beginning of the book to the effect that she has taken poetic license with the objective facts of her life. Not to do so is deceptive and duplicitous, and renders suspect the integrity of the entire journal. If May Sarton could lie about solitude and celibacy, what else has she lied about? Why even call it a journal if she seeks to avail herself of the privileges of fiction?

There is an ethical issue at stake here, it seems to me. Thousands of women have regarded May Sarton as a mentor, a role model and teacher of life, and now we discover that some of what she wrote is simply not true. I don't know. Perhaps it's old-fashioned of me to insist on a verifiable correlation between word and thing. "Lighten up, Marlene," I've been told. "People don't always mean what they say, or say what they mean." Perhaps not. But writers ought to. And I think that all of us—not only writers—ought to use words carefully. For all its shortcomings, language is our main mode of communication. If we say what we don't mean, and mean what we don't say, we demean its value, lead each other astray, and do harm to our relationships.

Now, how does this affect my own writing in this journal? I will surely say—either at the beginning of the journal or in an entry, perhaps this is it—that the text has been edited and condensed and that some names have been altered to protect the person's privacy. But I will try to be very clear about what liberties I take in the text, and I will not knowingly distort either the truth or the facts (which are not the same thing).

I don't imagine that any of the journals written for publication or even those published after the fact are exact reproductions of the original, spontaneous journal text. But there is a qualitative difference, it seems to me, between editing for clarity and gracefulness and perhaps even condensing several entries into one, and consciously creating a fiction—creating an utterly false impression about one of the journal's prominent themes. In Sarton's case, it was the issue of her solitude and celibacy. I suspect that Anne Truitt,

Burghild Nina Holzer, and Anne Lamott all rewrote and edited their respective journals for publication. But I also assume that the actual content of those journals has been as honestly represented as they could do it. That is the basic assumption we make about a published journal, it seems to me. As much as I have loved May Sarton's work over the years, she has broken faith with her readers in a serious fashion.

May 21st

Last week I read Carolyn Heilbrun's new book, *The Last Gift of Time: Life Beyond Sixty.* It is a lovely collection of her reflections on living during "the last decades of life," written, it seems to me, with a little more irony than her earlier books. Unpretentious and honest, it is full of wry humor and intelligent goodwill. Her heart is wide open. And she is beautiful. The photo of her on the book jacket shows an older woman with a wise and bemused smile, someone with whom you'd instantly like to have dinner and a long chat.

Much of what Heilbrun writes has to do with paring down to essentials. She describes her own process of dropping socially constructed affectations of femininity such as dresses, high heels, and other forms of gendered clothing that constrict women's freedom of movement. Why not dress for comfort and practicality, she asks, and give up trying to make ourselves into paragons of acquiescent femininity? As she donates her dresses to a women's shelter and rebuilds her wardrobe, she reflects,

> While I could never be called fashionable . . . at least my
> clothing was within the confines of the acceptable. I had
> abjured dresses and, above all, panty hose, discovered
> catalogs and a dressmaker, and learned to live with the
> knowledge that whatever I did and wherever I was
> going, I would be comfortable from my feet up.[33]

I saw Heilbrun at the Graduate Center in Manhattan about five years ago, when she was being honored for her work in women's studies after her dramatic resignation from Columbia University in protest against gender bias in their hiring practices. A striking figure in her royal blue suit, she was thoughtful, full of humor and kindness and that subversive intelligence, so elegant and wicked at once. Perhaps that kind of beauty—one's own unique beauty that has nothing to do with societal norms—takes time to grow into. And, of course, it has to do with the inner being, that quality of intelligent loving-kindness that radiates out and draws us in. Who isn't hungry to bask in that glow?

May 27th

The weeks between teaching terms often have an easy grace. There isn't that unsettled sense of writing in fits and starts between preparing for class, teaching, and grading that I feel once the semester is underway. These days, too few alas, have instead a quality of expansiveness that makes me want to do three or four things at once. Maybe even embark on a new project. It's a wonderfully luxurious way of working.

Lately I have been thinking about the role of homemaking in our fast-paced modern lives. One thing is for certain: in our rightful and necessary quest for economic equity and a public voice and presence, "something's lost and something's gained," in the words of Joni Mitchell's much-loved song. What's gained is clear: some measure of progress toward equal opportunity for women and the social recognition that derives from involvement in public life. What's lost is more elusive, insidious, even. There's no one home to tend the hearth; indeed, there is literally no one home-making. Relieved to be rising in the ranks of the gainfully employed at last, we discover that Athena's gain (goddess of wisdom and protector of cities) is Hestia's loss (goddess of hearth and home).

At the end of the day, what we go home to is not the welcoming aroma of a freshly prepared meal shared with dear familiars, but a kitchen full of appliances and gadgets, the better to expedite dinner-on-the-run before we head out to meet our personal trainer at the gym or rush to yet another committee meeting. Who wants to spend the evening inside a home-that-isn't, after all? No wonder then that invitations for intimate dinners in private homes occur so rarely these days. No wonder, to quote Marion Woodman's words slightly out of context, that "no one is receiving anyone these days." Perhaps I am belaboring the point, but it strikes me as profound. Self and home. If both are empty, there's no possibility of welcoming another. In order for a guest to be received, there must be a home, and someone consciously inhabiting it.

By no means am I saying that this task should revert to women; we have tended the hearth ever since fire was discovered, and I don't want to be forced back into the cave. But we do, for the most part, seem to know more intuitively than men do how to make a home for ourselves and those we love. Perhaps we could help our men to cultivate their own inner Hestia and share the loving labors involved, although I'm not sure exactly how this would be done. But I want to live in a real home, not a convenient rest station. I value, even cherish, the small tasks of homemaking that provide refuge and sanctuary, comfort and warmth. If Steve and I can "home-make" together, so much the better.

May 28th

Everything in our society seems to run counter to simple living. All of our human interactions are arranged to obscure so many of our authentic needs, such as the need for comfort and reassurance, for time to think and reflect on our lives, our need to be seen as we really are, and our creaturely need for freedom of bodily movement and sensuous experience. In their places we have set our sights on external rewards: social recognition and prestige, fame and fortune. But these are largely "grown-up" substitutes for what our bodies and souls really yearn for: love, freedom, kinship with other beings, bodily comfort, creative expression, pleasure in the present moment.

Too often we scramble frantically to meet the secondary needs while the real ones go unaddressed, because we feel apologetic, ashamed of our "primal" neediness. We feel we ought to have progressed beyond those needs by now, as if we were recalcitrant adults who, in the presence of steak and potatoes, stubbornly cling to the comfort of baby food. But the truth is that no amount of external recognition can give us the visceral reassurance provided by a caring human touch. No impressive job title or professional achievement can make our bodies feel loved.

How beautifully Etty Hillesum's journal gets to the heart of this conflict and how clear she was about what mattered most to her. Although the early pages of her journal are filled with self-exhortation to practice greater discipline in her daily affairs, she was keenly aware of the heart and soul of her life, of what she hungered for and how best to satisfy that hunger. More surprisingly, she was equally attuned to those around her, their joys and sorrows, their generosity and pettiness. "I believe I have gradually managed to attain the simplicity for which I have always longed," she confided to her journal on July 21, 1942. This she wrote as her familiar world was brutally being stripped away and the reality of her family's deportation to Auschwitz seemed more and more likely. "I still believe I have an inner regulator, which warns me every time I take the wrong path by bringing on a 'depression,'" she reflected. "If only I remain honest and open with myself and determined enough to become what I must be and to do what my conscience demands, then everything will turn out all right."[34] And perhaps it did, although not the way those of us who love her writing would have preferred. She died at Auschwitz on November 30, 1943.

. . . 1:45 p.m.

It seems to me that simplicity is related to humility. My dictionary of word origins tells me that "humble" means "close to the ground" and comes from the Latin *humilis* (low, lowly), a derivative of *humus* or "earth," related also to "human." "Humiliate" derives from the same origin.

Helen Luke says, "For the truly humble person no humiliation exists. It is impossible to humiliate him or for him to feel humiliation, for 'grades' and prestige, questions of his own merit or demerit, have no more meaning for him."[35] I don't know many people who live like that, myself included. But it's terribly important to be reminded that we can only be publicly humiliated if we subscribe to standards and values imposed from outside ourselves. If, like Etty Hillesum, we allow the still, small inner voice to speak our heart's truth and stay faithful to what we hear, there can be no such thing as humiliation. Instead, we are *humble,* close to the ground, to our origin—to our beloved earth.

May 29th

In *The Playing Self,* Steve's colleague, Alberto Melucci, writes:

> The surfeit of possibilities available to us far exceeds what we can effectively cope with and utilize, and our everyday life is choked with opportunities which we are unable to seize. . . . Insufficient time, the necessity to choose, and the renunciation of many possibilities that any action entails seem to generate many of the central difficulties and hardships experienced in everyday life. Complexity creates pressures in people's lives, to which they respond by attempting to adjust. Efforts are often frustrated, and the failure provokes suffering. . . . We cannot be everywhere, we cannot be everything, we often end up living only in a succession of discrete moments.[36]

As a "negative definition" of simplicity, I think this description of the modern condition is accurate. To top it off, we are constantly hammered with reminders of that "surfeit of possibilities" through advertising and the media. Not allowed the luxury of our present commitment, we are endlessly bombarded with claims of new and improved, updated and more efficient versions, whether in relation to possessions, career possibilities, or even personal relationships.

For what was my sense of fragmentation and angry rushing on Tuesday but the sense that I ought to do everything at once, make great progress in all of my projects—and all on the same day! "Choked with opportunities," all of them worthy, I didn't know what to do first, where to direct my energies. "Too many activities, and people, and things," Anne Morrow Lindbergh reflected. "For it is not merely the trivial which clutters our lives but the important as well."[37] So I promised myself an hour or two on this journal, an hour on teaching preparation, an hour to proofread Steve's paper, an hour for the gym and another to walk, and an hour to make some telephone calls. But I never really surrendered myself to any of these activities because my mind was always jumping ahead to the next hour and the next task, as if I really *had* to do it all that day. Talk about fragmentation and a surfeit of possibilities!

This is why it's so important that we be clear about what is most important to us out of many possible claims on our time. And why self-knowledge is so crucial. It's also why any kind of conscious long-term commitment is so subversive in our age. Take a fifty-year marriage, for example. Imagine all the "new and improved versions" that have been passed up if the partners have been "faithful" to each other throughout half a century, all the opportunities for diverting and pleasurable dalliances along the way. Think of the willingness to stick by each other through thick and thin, to keep "choosing again what I chose before,"[38] in the words of Wendell Berry. Think of the faith and commitment required to keep alive a relationship based on more than mere habit and inertia.

It also occurs to me that what Alberto Melucci is doing in elegant and abstract terms—exploring how we negotiate between the endless complex possibilities open to us and our desire for a coherent and meaningful life—is also my intention in writing this journal, except that I am doing it in concrete and practical down-to-earth terms, with all the gritty details, flaws, and inconsistencies of a specific life in progress. And what he says about the painful frustrations of our modern experience of time is equally true of all our experience. We are constantly called on to negotiate between the many and the one. "We cannot be everywhere, we cannot be everything," indeed. But we often drive ourselves crazy in the attempt.

May 30th

I have found that on days like this, when I get off to a late start and feel that the day has already gotten away from me, the best thing I can do is to stop and take several slow, deep breaths. Then I begin to move around the house in a very deliberate way, with great care and attention, breathing deeply all the while and resisting the urge to make up for lost time. If I don't remember to do this I get breathless, trying to catch up to where a critical voice says I "should have been," as if I can expand the remaining hours and make each one hold more than a normal hour can.

But who or what is that idealized efficient self I'm trying to live up to? Where does that judgment come from, telling me I ought to have accomplished more, be further along and use time more efficiently—especially when there's no external deadline to meet? And when I have long decided that regular workouts at the gym are just as important as other priorities in my life, for example.

The older I get, it seems, the more value I place on movement and exercise. My body is my home. I want to give it every chance to remain healthy for many decades and into old age. After so many years spent hating it, then in wary coexistence, I am finally beginning to make my peace with it—I think, I hope—with its sags and stretch marks as well as the rich round curves I find lovely in other women. Curiously, in cherishing Steve's body as I do, I have been freed to love my own. And in sensing how much comfort my arms can offer others, my body has become sacred to me, at last.

In my twenties it seemed to take more of an effort to be serious about my commitment to its well-being. Now exercise simply takes its important place in my life, without much thought or discipline required. It's an integral part of my day, like brewing the morning pot of coffee, spending time with Steve, and writing in my journal. I devote so many hours to my mind, heart, and soul every day, that I don't think a couple of hours a day for exercising and preparing healthy meals is extravagant. It boosts my well-being on so many levels.

Twenty years ago in Vancouver, Kathie and I would sometimes make a day of it; we'd set out at noon and walk for many miles and hours, stopping for cappuccino and muffins along the way. That became our favorite way of visiting, sharing intimacies as we faced each other across the table or booth, then walking another mile or two to let the conversation and our emotions settle. By nightfall, we'd have a pleasant sense of exhaustion as we made a final stop at Simpatico's or Orestes' restaurant for a well-deserved chicken souvlaki.

Even now, I love the challenge of very long walks in the city. It's approximately a hundred blocks from Zabar's, at 81st and Broadway, to South Ferry—at least two hours of very brisk walking. I generally do it alone. I don't know anyone else who would enjoy it or take the time, and the streets of Manhattan are so crowded and noisy that trying to carry on a conversation while dodging other pedestrians and the infamous New York City cabs would be frustrating and downright dangerous, in any case. Along the way, I often duck into a restaurant to rest my feet and have a drink. Sometimes I write in my journal. Even while I don't want to live in the City, it's exhilarating to walk there, my senses saturated with too many sights and sounds, smells and bodies. I don't even miss having a walking partner. Better to allow my thoughts and sensory impressions to float freely. Sometimes I lose track of where I am, and have no memory of having walked the last ten or fifteen blocks. Then I round the corner, and suddenly New York Harbor gleams blue and silver before my eyes.

May 31st

I just returned from the local butcher shop, having purchased the summer's worth of meat, mainly chicken, during their weeklong sale. For $50 I bought fifteen pounds of chicken pieces for curry and cacciatore, ten pounds of chicken patties, five pounds of lean ground sirloin for meat sauce, and a piece of London broil to simmer with Mum's sauerkraut. This will last us well into the fall since we're eating less meat these days.

I saved countless hours, and probably again as much money, by buying everything during one trip, and on sale. How simple, how easy, to save $50 plus five or ten future shopping hours. I wonder why everyone wouldn't take advantage of such easy-to-implement time and money saving strategies. Tonight I'll spend an hour or two skinning the chicken and preparing it for the freezer. Again it's the little freezer that makes this bulk food shopping possible.

June 2nd

Last night Arts and Entertainment televised an hour-long biography of Mother Teresa. How can anyone's heart radiate so much love? All the volunteers who go to India to help out (she has established homes in 120 countries) say, faces aglow, that they receive more back from those they serve than they give. This does suggest that at bottom people long for a chance to do something meaningful for others and to tap more deeply into their own physical, emotional, and spiritual resources. So little in our culture invites a joyful, openhearted giving of oneself that we yearn for an opportunity to affirm our common humanity. I can understand so well the desire to go to India and be part of it.

At the same time, as I was watching it occurred to me how many opportunities there are, in our less exotic everyday lives, to extend kindness and compassion to those around us. How many possibilities there are to live with that same heightened consciousness of purpose, here and now. In our harried, humdrum daily lives it's not so easy to keep our shared humanity in the forefront and to regard every person we encounter as a "child of God." But how terribly important it is, in an age where respect and simple human courtesy have been replaced with envy and adulation of power.

Her biographer told a story involving Mother Teresa's insistence on reaching a group of handicapped children who'd been abandoned in the middle of the war zone in Lebanon. Hearing of her arrival, all sides put their deadly antagonisms on hold and ceased their fighting, out of respect for her. Who else could bring a war to halt by their very presence? Perhaps Nelson Mandela and Mahatma Gandhi, but no one else that I can think of.

How gently she cradled a skeletal, misshapen child of perhaps six or eight years, gazing into its eyes with undiluted love, where many might have felt an embarrassed mixture of pity and revulsion. "A child of God." And talk about living a simple life. When she left the cloistered life, Mother Teresa resolved to wear homespun saris and carry no more than five rupees in her pocket, so as to share the lot of the poor she served. When she received the Nobel Peace Prize in 1979, she promptly canceled the banquet scheduled in her honor on the grounds that the $7000 saved would feed 400 Indians for a year! Now *that* is a sense of right proportion. What psychic freedom, not to be encumbered with excess material goods, credit cards, and everything else that accompanies our modern western lifestyle. And to be absolutely clear that in serving the "poorest of the poor," one is serving God.

Mother Teresa never sleeps more than four hours a night, rising early to witness the Calcutta dawn in prayer. Surely there is something more than merely human energy that sustains this woman. Her life moves me like few others do, and if we go to India, I want to go and see the work for myself. From one woman with a clear sense of her life's purpose, the work grew to a dozen, then hundreds—and now four thousand Sisters. It is no overstatement to say that the world has been changed by her fierce and uncompromising love.

Another scene I loved occurred when her biographer asked if she ever felt humiliation (in the conventional sense, not as Helen Luke uses the word). Mother Teresa laughed and said, "Oh yes, many times. Right now, for example, being interviewed like this!" She felt humiliated, not by living in the midst of incredible filth or by working with throw-away people in the gutters of the poorest city in the world, but by being made the focus of close scrutiny and curious attention. What a complete reversal of the world's prevailing values.

One of the men who works with her said, "When Mother Teresa looks at you, she doesn't see you; she sees *into you*." And, since she looks with the eyes of love, what she sees is nothing less than a "child of God," someone deserving of love, no matter how wretched or nasty. That is how I would like to see people too. It brings to mind a beautiful passage in Drew Leder's book, where he quotes from the writing of a Hindu swami Ramdas.

> Just as a flower gives out its radiance to whomever approaches or uses it, so love from within us radiates toward everybody and manifests as spontaneous service. . . . When we feed, clothe, and attend on anybody, we feel like doing all these things to our own body,

for which we do not expect any return or praise or commendation, because all bodies are our own; for, we as the all-pervading Atman or Spirit reside in all bodies.[39]

What a beautiful acknowledgment of our relatedness.

June 4th

Is there any aspect of simple living that I haven't dealt with to date in this journal? My thoughts keep returning to Mother Teresa, and I suppose I haven't written much about spiritual simplicity, or spirituality *and* simplicity. I think that's partly because even twenty-two years after breaking with evangelical Christianity—exactly half my lifetime ago—I'm still leery of using religious vocabulary. I don't see my spirituality as a separate part of my life, in any case. Although I do not use religious language to describe it, my spirituality infuses everything that I am and do; I don't even know how to discuss it on its own. I feel it in my relationship with nature—the ocean and mountains, and especially trees and flowers—with other people, certainly with Steve and my mother, in the Workshop, and in my closest friendships. I remember reading (although I don't recall who said this) that "Attention is the sincerest form of prayer," and I know for me, this is true.

This is at the heart of my yearning to connect at a soul level with other people and my lifelong intuition that, religion and dogma aside, the only thing that matters is love. All my life I have wanted to be a channel of love, perhaps even more so after my break with the German Baptist Church. Despite my sometimes blunt and critical tongue, that desire persists. Before that break, I felt the pressure to reflect God's love—a daunting task and one I always felt inadequate to carry out—and to "witness" to all the lost souls around me. As the filter of evangelical Christianity gradually fell from my eyes, I became free to regard people on their own terms, to try to understand their beliefs and convictions, to engage with them as fellow searchers rather than as potential converts. I remember both how terrifying and how exhilarating that was. After so many years of regarding people as either "saved" and "one of us" or as one of the "un-saved" masses, to finally be free to perceive them without that absolute judgment and certainty of my own moral rightness was earth-shaking. I can only compare it to moving from black-and-white perception to a sudden glimpse of the full spectrum of the rainbow.

But for many reasons and in many ways it's so difficult to really see another person without the filter of our own projections. It's the rare person who is really able to do it. I don't know many people who can clear out enough space to allow another in. When we meet someone who offers us that depth of attention, we fall in love with them. It's the quality of eye contact that signals this kind of attentiveness, the steadiness of their gaze, the repose of their body, and the quiet watchfulness to another's gestures, shifting moods and emotions. I imagine this is why people go to psychotherapists; they yearn for such undivided attention. How sad that we often seem unable to give it to each other.

A line in my "daily thoughts for women" reads, "The best gift we can give each other is rapt attention to each other's existence." What a beautiful way to put it. Listening is such an underrated activity, more often understood as the passive absence of speech rather than as the vital and sometimes exhausting process that it is. Genuine listening takes an open heart, great clarity, tremendous focus and energy, and the readiness to set one's own agenda aside and really receive another person. I think this accounts for the glazed look people sometimes exhibit when trapped in a one-sided conversation they would sooner escape. Just how hungry we are to be listened to has been evident to Steve and me after spending a long time listening to another person, when upon parting, they say how much they have enjoyed meeting us, although we have hardly said anything. Over the years Steve and I have found that good listeners are very rare. Most people would rather be talking.

Meanwhile, I am reading Helen Luke in preparation for Wednesday's workshop. It is always so good, so important to be reminded to dwell in the feminine realm, to value what is receptive, responsive, quiet, and hidden as much as the outward heroic quest of the masculine. Luke writes about "receptive devotion" and "creative resonance" as quintessential feminine qualities that are not recognized, much less valued in this culture.[40] I love the term "creative resonance" because it evokes the vital receptivity and active responsiveness that can "hear women into their own speech," in the words of Nelle Morton. A listening ear had to be present in order for the Word to be received, and Morton sees here, "a complete reversal of the going logic . . . a depth hearing that takes place before speaking—a hearing that is more than acute listening. A hearing that is a direct transitive verb that evokes speech—new speech that has never been spoken before."[41] At best, this is what takes place in the workshop, I think.

June 5th

I'm not yet at peace about the "child issue," as we have referred to it over the years. I don't feel desperate at the thought that we might not have a child, but I'm not neutral either. I want to have one. And in the circumstances we envision, it should be possible for us to write and to raise a child at the same time. Still, I have felt all along that if it's meant to happen, it will, without high-tech intervention. And if it doesn't, I hope that I can accept that as an answer from the Goddess, deal with any grief I feel, and channel my love wherever it's needed most.

Having no children may make my life less complicated on a practical level, but the whole issue has been anything but simple to resolve. The factor of choice imposes a dimension of complexity that our mothers generally did not face, albeit a welcome one; I wouldn't want to go back to earlier options. The assumption in previous generations has been that marriage and children went together. Couples without children were more often childless as a result of infertility problems than by choice. Now we can choose. Women can study and work, pursue a wide variety of careers and travel the world, devote ourselves to causes we believe in, and arrange our lives to suit ourselves. But often we can't do that *and* have a family, as men have always managed to do. Since many of us want both, how do we orchestrate a meaningful life for ourselves—in which we can have it all? There's nothing simple about this challenge and yet, in one form or another, we all must face it.

June 7th

In *Your Money or Your Life,* Joe Dominguez and Vicki Robin tell of a man who swore he could eat well each day for the price of a pack of cigarettes, which was then $1.45. Just to prove his case he did it for a month and came out $8 ahead. Out of curiosity I decided to make a list of what could be purchased for that amount of money and discovered he was right.

I don't know what he ate in the course of that month but, shopping carefully, for $45 I could purchase more than enough food to sustain me. Here is what I came up with: A pound each of soybeans, chickpeas, lentils, brown rice, oats, raisins, butter, coffee, peanut butter, and sour cream; two pounds of pasta, onions, broccoli, and homemade meat sauce; several pounds of carrots, cabbage, squash, chicken, bananas; five pounds of apples and potatoes; a pint of olive oil, a gallon of milk, two dozen eggs, eight ounces of good chocolate (an essential food group), and some homemade bread and cookies. The key would be to avoid refined foods, which are always more expensive and less nutritious, in any case, and to eat very little meat.

If I had to live with this budget—as in essence I did as a student in England—I'd focus on soups and stews in the winter and salads in the summer. I'd be healthy and well-nourished at the end of the month, most likely with food left over. There is something exhilarating in the realization that one could eat well for a month on the amount that can easily be spent on a dinner out. And it explains why Nellie's friend and her husband can live in Victoria on next to nothing. Since they own their little apartment and don't run a car, they basically need money only for groceries. He is an aspiring artist who has not sold his work to date, and she collects and restores old and antique dolls. Because they are clear about their priorities, they have tremendous freedom to live as they please. Every now and then she works for a few months, and that provides them with cash flow for the rest of the year.

June 10th

After dinner last night we walked on the boardwalk. As always, it was wondrously calming. The sound of the waves and the wind coming off the ocean puts things into perspective and reminds me of something larger than my anxious preoccupations of the day. I want to stay there, to gaze at the endless expanse of shimmering water and to feel the vast openness that stretches far beyond what my eyes can see. It provides such relief from the petty provincialism of life on Staten Island.

There by the ocean I do feel the simplicity of being alive, with my beloved Steve at my side, striding briskly, his long legs taking two steps for every three of mine. Occasionally I notice someone scribbling away or engrossed in a book. One day I will take my journal and stay as long as I like, and write for hours to the rhythm of the waves. I would love to have a workshop there as well. I think we would write differently by water.

June 16th

I met Claudia and Peter for a picnic in Central Park yesterday. Because of the tensions between us during the past week, my heart was not in it. I felt torn, tired of the long-term strains and stresses of the relationship. I was relieved when I left them to shop at Zabar's before meeting Steve. Given our history of misunderstandings and mutual resentments, I can only think it was, as Steve suggested, for the sake of peace in the extended family that I even chose to meet them at all.

Sometimes I feel as if we speak different languages. We might as well, given how different our aims in communicating seem to be. It seems to me that Peter protects himself with wit and irony, and rarely shows his true feelings. Claudia is more difficult to deal with. Steve thinks she projects her unresolved anger toward her family onto me. I've often wondered about that myself when things go wrong between us and I can't understand her behavior. Or maybe it would be more accurate to say that I can't decode it. It's as if she has a clear script of how everyone should behave in any given circumstance, and I just can't seem to break the code. She seems to alternately blow hot and cold, as if she's trying to keep us guessing. I'm tired of putting so much emotional energy into that relationship. I'm tired of dreaming about it so often, although I suspect that the dreams are trying to tell me something about my own part in the problem.

Why is it so difficult to keep the channels of communication open, even among people who care about each other? What I long for most is intimacy with others, to be allowed to share my interior landscape with them and to be invited into theirs. But that doesn't seem to be what Claudia and Peter want. I think they prefer a more casual and distanced mode of relating to people, something more sophisticated. That's probably why we're at cross-purposes in our attempts to communicate; we're looking for different things. In a sense we really *are* speaking different languages.

Emotionally, I'm having a difficult time releasing it. I still want to believe that with open hearts and sufficient good will, we can work out our differences and misunderstandings. But I can't do it alone, and there's no reason to believe that they want a less socialized, more authentic relationship. Sadly, I will have to let it go, at least for now.

Last night we had an informal dinner and discussion of group process at the Upper East Side home of Claire, one of Steve's friends from the Dialogue group. My apprehension concerning "high-level" socializing—psychiatrists, psychologists, psychoanalysts, some with several published books to their names—abates, I've discovered, when I can see the group as composed of individuals, each with his or her own strengths and vulnerabilities, any of whom I could happily have a one-on-one conversation with. I think there's a tendency in situations where I'm a little apprehensive to experience it as "the group" and myself, and I have to remind myself that for the person next to me, *I* am part of that collective entity, the group, just as they are for me.

When I can consciously relax, breathe, look around, and listen, I feel comfortable, whether or not I'm participating verbally. When I remind myself that I have no agenda and nothing to prove and that I'd simply like to know who these people are, I don't feel performance anxiety any longer. On our walk afterward, I told Steve that it's wonderful and somehow surprising to feel at forty-three—so *this* is who I am. I'm more at peace with myself than I have been in the past, not looking to other people as much for affirmation and approval. Of course there's still a long way to go.

June 19th

There is something beautifully simple about sharing one's life with another person. When I was single in Vancouver in the late 1970s, I was often lonely, even though I had several close friends and a wide circle of acquaintances. Doing freelance work in arts administration, I was alone most days. It's different now. I may crave more social interaction and external stimulation from time to time, but I don't experience that bone-deep existential loneliness anymore.

When I wake up in the morning, it's to the sounds of birdsong and Steve's gentle snoring. Our bodies have grown into one, so much so that when he is away for a few days my body has to relocate itself on the bed. When I go out for the day, it's always with the knowledge that he will be there when I return, happy to see me and hear about my day. After a disappointing class, I hash it out with him before bed and fall asleep relieved.

There is nothing sweeter or more comforting than falling asleep next to one's beloved. Whatever the irritations or petty grievances of the day, there isn't a night that our bodies don't find peace in lying next to each other, instinctively entraining our breathing into a single calming rhythm. There are many times when I yearn for a wider community of kindred spirits; no two people can be everything to each other. But there is something blessed about having a companion in life, someone whose happiness is as important as my own and to whom I have freely pledged my love and care and the deepest honesty I'm capable of. Someone who is there, when night falls, with the balm of tenderness for the bruises of the day.

I remember saying throughout my twenties that even if I never met "the right man," I would create a rich and meaningful life for myself. And I believe that I would have, even if there was loneliness at times. But once my life grew intertwined with Steve's, even with all the uncertainty and conflict of the early years—could I ever get used to New York and his children, would we get married, have a child, move back to Vancouver?—I began to know the richness of having a companion in life and of gaining a new perspective, at once double and shared. During the almost twelve years that we have been together, I have not experienced that penetrating loneliness of old, that nagging thirst for intimate relationship that builds intensity like the absence of cool water in an unrelenting heat spell. Sometimes I have felt that lifelong monogamy is an artificial and unnecessary social restraint. But more often I find an elegant simplicity in the shared commitment to create a life that will encompass, with equal weight of importance, the needs and desires of two people whose souls are at home with each other.

June 21st

I am sitting on the living room couch. It's very hot and humid today, 83 degrees inside, and I will turn the air conditioning on soon. We try not to use it until mid-afternoon, in order to limit the freon we release into the atmosphere.

On the weekend I am often restless if we haven't planned any social engagements. The feeling of being cut off and isolated reminds me of being home alone on a Saturday night in my twenties, convinced that everyone else in the world was out on a romantic dinner date. This was more fantasy than reality, of course, but even knowing that many others were sitting at home on a lovely summer evening and feeling just as alone as I was did not help at all. I wanted to be out in the midst of things, kicking up my heels, in every sense.

Today—early Saturday afternoon—I'm glad we don't have anything planned. The past few weeks have been so busy—work, long-distance consultations with Mum's surgeon about her upcoming carotid artery operation, social gatherings, classes, the workshop and book group—that I need some time quietly at home, to collect myself.

Sometimes I'm so far from being able to flow with time, I realize. I want to "manage" my life and create a harmonious balance of writing and teaching, friendship, music, exercise—all the components of my life. When I experience an imbalance—too much of one and too little of another—I'm discontent. Perhaps it's my Libra nature manifesting itself, always hoping to find the perfect proportion. True simplicity, I am sure, would entail being fully present in *each* moment, whatever it brings. Not fretting about what ought to be, what I'd like to have in my life, or what comes next. But when I'm feeling isolated and discontent, this is hard to remember. It's all too easy to fall into magical thinking: "If only I were/I could/I had . . . my life would be better and I'd be happier."

June 22nd

If simple living involves knowing one's path and being true to it, I ought to be largely content. I write, teach, work with women, exercise, share my life with Steve, travel (although not as much as I'd like), and generally do what I want with my life.

My multifaceted vocation suits me very well. Teaching provides external structure, the weekly setpoints around which I plan my other activities. It also gives expression to my extroverted side. Communicating with students satisfies my need for meaningful human interaction, affirms my ability to share knowledge with others, and makes good use of my leadership qualities. It also gives me professional colleagues and provides a sense of belonging, even if only marginally, to an academic and intellectual community. And I suspect that it adds to my credence as a writer and workshop leader to be teaching at the university level. Although this is not why I teach, strategically it is probably a good idea to have an academic affiliation.

The second branch of my vocation, the Women's Journal Workshop, is my own creation and therefore especially rewarding. I imagined and loved it into existence with endless unstinting hours of planning, shaping, and organizing. The Workshop is a kind of cottage industry. I do it all myself, from designing the brochures and addressing the envelopes, choosing the theme and shaping the day's writing, to baking the cakes, setting up the living room chairs, and lighting the candles. Everything related to the Workshop reflects who I am, what I believe in and love. In turn, the Workshop calls on all that is best in me: My ability to listen with focused and loving attention. Warmth and readiness to nurture. Embodied presence and willingness to serve others. Sensitivity and discernment, intuition and empathy, spontaneity and love of beauty. Here I am teacher, writer, mother, friend, therapist, mentor, facilitator, administrator, cook, and more. The Workshop keeps my heart wide open, allows me to teach effortlessly from the deepest center of my being, where heart and mind and soul all nourish each other. This is the most holistic work I do. Unlike university teaching where intellect rules, everything I am counts here.

And not least, it allows me to share one of the most important dimensions of my life—my journal habit—with others who feel this passion themselves or, at least, are receptive to it. It provides another form of that essential and loving connection with women that has always sustained me and allows me to help other women struggle to find their own voices, just as I have struggled to find my own. The trust, intimacy, and unconditional acceptance in the Workshop create a communion that I don't experience anywhere else but in my closest friendships, and that many of the women who come have described as unprecedented. That's why, even while it slowly expands, I don't want it to get too big. I fear that closeness might be threatened by numbers.

Finally, there is my writing. I can't imagine my life without it. Writing is my best friend and loyal companion, my solitude and my inner life. It is where I discover what I think and feel and believe, and where I articulate the questions that I "attempt to live," in the words of Rilke. It's also where I receive answers. Writing brings together my logical and linear capacities with my musicality and sense of rhythm; my love of ideas and of emotional connections. Since I don't remember a time when I wasn't writing, I can't even know all of the ways in which it has shaped the woman I have become. It has probably affected the syntax of my thoughts in ways I don't even understand.

And maybe writing is also my means of embracing the mystery of life and my mode of prayer. Over and over again, it brings me face to face with my shadow and forces me to confront my greatest weaknesses and flaws. It replenishes my inner well and allows me to return to my friends, to the Workshop, to my students with a fresh perspective and renewed loving-kindness.

While my Workshop and college teaching keep me connected to the world, my writing keeps me in touch with myself.

June 23rd

Perhaps it's true in any relationship, that it is often small every-day moments that mean the most and express the unique character of that union. What I cherish most about my life with Steve are not the big things. It's our daily walks on the boardwalk when we talk about our work-in-progress or our anticipated move to the West Coast. It's lying on the sofa after dinner with my feet in Steve's lap or his in mine; falling asleep in his arms as he tenderly strokes my back; preparing dinner when he has been out for the day, and knowing that at any moment he'll walk through the front door. Small, shared habits that make up the warp and woof of our quiet life together; how precious they become over the years.

Given the amount of time we spend together, it's odd how seldom we quarrel. Time seems to have mellowed us both and lengthened our respective fuses. We've become more tolerant of each other's weaknesses and don't take them so personally anymore. And, as we often say, we just don't know—at forty-three and fifty-four—how much time we will have together. Life is too short to indulge in petty resentments. Not that we never succumb, but it seems to me that we're able to get out of it much more quickly than we did eight or ten years ago.

June 24th

How curious that when we anticipate meeting someone, even a close friend whom we haven't seen in some time, first thoughts often seem to concern how they will perceive us. Will she notice the gray in my hair? Will he still find me attractive? Will they think I've aged? As if physical appearance is the final measure of our value.

I'm embarrassed to admit that when Laël rang from Paris to say she was coming to New York and wanted to get together, one of my reactions was: When we saw each other last in Vancouver four years ago, I was at my heaviest weight ever. I'm so glad that I've lost weight. Here we are, two women who were close friends for years, intelligent and creative souls both, and body image is still an issue for me as we arrange to get together. Not that I wouldn't have wanted to see her in any case, but my pleasure would have been tinged with self-consciousness, even a faint sense of shame.

No matter how much I want to love and accept my body at any weight, I can't seem to shake the feeling that when I'm fifty pounds overweight I am not myself. Heavy, I feel loose, undefined, and out of focus. My real self seems blurred, like a pencil drawing smudged beyond easy recognition. I feel the awkward shame of having betrayed my own body, my greed and lack of self-control exposed for all the world to see. Weight must be the last taboo in this culture, the last righteous prejudice, directed not least by ourselves against our own bodies.

These feelings are no doubt enhanced by the fact that I don't feel physically well when I'm heavy. Assaulted by food allergies, skin problems, and various minor aches and pains, my body is sluggish, reluctant to move around. And, of course, there are many health risks associated with carrying excess weight after the age of forty. When I recall what that was like, I'm so grateful things are heading in a healthier direction.

June 25th

Steve trimmed my hair yesterday. This time, thankfully, two inches in theory turned out to be two inches in practice; last time he lopped off five. It's not a professional job, but it looks fine, and will carry me through until my planned consultation with a hairstylist in Vancouver next month.

How much time, hassle, and money have I saved over the years by not frequenting beauty salons, I wonder? It must be hundreds of hours and thousands of dollars by now. It took Steve about ten minutes to trim it, and me another five to clean up. I saved at least an hour and a half, and $25.

In forty-three years I have never colored or permed my hair. Now I am contemplating a big step. With a little more gray than I'd like, I'm thinking of going to a good hairstylist this summer and having my hair restored to its former brown glory. I'm vain enough to want my dark hair to stay dark for a few years longer, but I have no intention of paying $75 every six weeks to keep it that way, so I want to learn how to maintain it myself. Then again, maybe I'll decide to go gray after all. There's something appealing about simply allowing nature to take its course. Time will tell.

. . . 8:30 p.m., during the workshop

I believe that having the Workshop in my home is another way of keeping things simple. It means that I don't have to pack up my materials and coffee pot and head out to an impersonal and sterile conference room, and women always comment on how safe, comfortable, and nurtured they feel in my living room, with the huge pine journal bookcase just around the corner in the dining room. In my own home I am serene and relaxed. If I were to hold the Workshop elsewhere it would immediately become more commercial and lose some of its intimacy and warmth.

Earlier today, as I prepared for tonight's session, I thought about how it is a labor of love, a ritual of caring. Each Wednesday I tidy the living room and dust, clean the bathroom and put out fresh towels, prepare the cake and drinks, set the table, and put out all the photocopied handouts. Finally, an hour before it begins, I get dressed and start making coffee. Then I put on music and read or write until people arrive, so that I'm calm and grounded when we begin. I never rush because I want the atmosphere to be serene and meditative as women arrive at the end of their hectic workdays.

There is comfort in knowing that every Wednesday evening the living room will hold a circle of women quietly writing their lives, exploring their inner realm, privately but in community. Comfort for me, as well as for them. And genuine comfort is a rare thing in our frantic world, I have discovered.

June 30th

Shuffling slowly, gingerly along on the boardwalk yesterday evening, less than forty-eight hours after injuring my back (ironically while lifting a heavy bag of organic produce out of the car), I felt immense gratitude for the physical well-being I enjoy and so often take for granted. There's nothing like a painful back problem to highlight my usual good health! Because I'm generally sturdy, I take it for granted much of the time, in a way that I don't, for example, take my relationship with Steve for granted. I have never suffered from chronic illness or fatigue and so my healthy day-to-day existence is still, to me, the norm. And, as Drew Leder points out in *The Absent Body*, when we are well, the body is invisible. It's only when illness or disease strikes, that it comes into view.

Then again, I don't entirely take it for granted. Several years ago when my mother commented that it was a shame my income didn't reflect all those expensive years of study, I told her that as long as Steve and I were both healthy and had enough of everything we needed, I really couldn't complain. Apparently she remembered that conversation for a long time, because she later quoted it back to me. It seems so clear to me that being healthy is the bottom line. What good is anything else—time, freedom, money, talent—without good health?

That's why, no matter how busy things get, I exercise regularly. It's why we take our daily regimen of vitamins and joined the Purple Dragon organic produce co-op. And it's also the reason why, deep down, I don't feel guilty about rarely using the alarm clock. Steve and I are two of the few people I know who are not sleep deprived. Now that I know getting enough sleep strengthens the immune system, I'm thoroughly enjoying our freedom to get eight hours a night.

As far as I'm concerned, this *is* the good life, just about as unstressed in most ways as it's possible to be in this day and age, and full of possibility and open horizons. I am so thankful. It's odd that I haven't written much on the topic of health in here. Perhaps it took my back pain to bring my body out of the shadow and back into view.

Later . . .

After eight months of writing this journal, I feel I'm beginning to understand more consciously the choices I have made and to appreciate that this is indeed the life I have invented, with its many blessings and occasional discontents.

Yes, we live in a rented house that is clearly beneath our means. We could live in a more beautiful environment and own a home with greater material comfort, even some luxury. Most couples in our position would probably do just that. Instead, we have lived here for almost eight years and will likely stay another three, until we're ready to relocate to the Pacific Northwest. But our three-bedroom main floor apartment meets our basic needs for space and comfort. It's a twelve minute drive to and from the College, five minutes to the ocean. We haven't had a rent increase since we moved in, although by the same token the landlord hasn't done anything to maintain the house, and it looks pretty shabby these days. All these years, we haven't faced the responsibilities or expenses of home ownership. The huge living room has provided an ideal space for my Workshop, and we've each had our own study, with adequate if not abundant space. Our dead-end street is fairly quiet most of the time (except when the teenager at the end of the block steers his motorized mini-car up and down the block for hours on end and nobody complains because he belongs to a Mob family!).

As Steve has pointed out, we certainly could eat out more often and in posher restaurants, go to the theater and concerts more frequently, and spend more money on clothes and travel if we were so inclined, but the truth is that we don't feel deprived. We decided several years ago that our priority is to own our home when we move, either free and clear or as nearly as possible, so for now we are happy to squirrel away as much of our income as we can. A night at the theater or Carnegie Hall, including a modest dinner, bridge tolls, and parking in Manhattan, can easily run over $200, so we are judicious in our consumption of high culture as well.

If all goes well, these choices will allow us to live comfortably enough in B. C., with Steve free to write full-time, and myself, at least half-time. If I also decide to do a little teaching, the additional income should allow us to travel occasionally and replace our car when required, especially if we drive our next car for fifteen years, as we have our trusty '86 Camry. There will be time to walk around the seawall in Stanley Park and hike in the mountains surrounding Vancouver. We'll invite friends over for musical evenings and lasagna, and we'll wander down to Granville Island Market for a late afternoon café latté. We'll enjoy the lifestyle I have long dreamed of, so I hope.

July 3rd

In her wonderful essay "Money and the Feminine Principle of Relatedness," Helen Luke writes:

> One cannot go back to the simple life until one has taken up the responsibility for money and learned the nature of exchange through both earning and paying. . . . As with every other collective problem, there can be no outer solution without the transformation of individuals. There is, therefore, the imperative need for each person to enter upon the hard way of scrutinizing with ever increasing consciousness his or her own personal attitudes to money.[42]

Tracing the origin of money back to the Roman goddess Moneta, in whose temple money was coined, Helen Luke tells us that because money is a symbolic means of exchange, it "belongs to the feminine principle of relatedness." Who would have imagined this? Because it has become an abstraction—the ancient gold coin replaced first by inherently worthless pieces of paper, and then by the modern plastic credit card—the financial world has always struck me as one of the most abstract and patriarchal domains of contemporary life. Everything can be bought—for a price. The original symbolism long since lost, money has become its own god. If television has replaced the family hearth, Wall Street has become the modern temple of choice.

It was not ever thus, Helen Luke tells us. Originally, the symbolic exchange of coinage for goods and services rendered had its own inherent dignity; each party recognized the other's common humanity and the value of what they had received. At a time when the global gap between "haves" and "have-nots" has reached unprecedented proportions, how far we have strayed from that. There is no dignity in the greed to amass fortunes, whether on the part of individuals or corporations. There is only the growing worship of the bottom line. And that respectful recognition of a symbolic exchange among human beings has deteriorated into the blind insistence that everything we undertake prove profitable.

July 7th

This summer, meal preparation has become very simple. I have gotten into the habit of cooking once a week, either Sunday or Monday. Then we eat whatever I've cooked throughout the week, supplemented with organic produce and fresh bread. Lately it was roast chicken one week followed by pasta with vegetables, chicken patties, and veggie burgers. This week it's vegetarian lasagna. On the remaining nights we might order in a pizza or pick up bagels and cold cuts. The preparation time is minimal, even with our daily organic salads. I wash the greens as soon as we get them—they stay fresh for a week—and then it's just a matter of piling other chopped and grated vegetables on top with some feta cheese or a handful of nuts.

In the course of my busier than usual summer, this seems to be a simple and efficient way to make sure we eat well. Steve doesn't enjoy spending time in the kitchen, and I don't want to devote an hour and a half to dinner every day either. Muffins and banana bread from the freezer take care of breakfast, and for lunch we have bread with a little cheese and fruit. I think we'll continue like this through the rest of the year.

Meanwhile I have begun to sort through my clothes but realize I'm not quite ready to get rid of absolutely everything I know I'll never wear again. The size nine black cotton dress I bought in Paris in 1977 and the Liberty cotton shirts I bought in England, also too small now, are dear reminders of times gone by, and for the moment, I can't bear to throw them out. This sorting will have to be a gradual process, no doubt gaining momentum as we draw nearer to our anticipated moving date. There are at least a dozen new items that I have never worn: blouses, skirts, dresses, pants. Those I can part with more readily.

I must admit that when I picture the closets half empty, my heart thrills. It would change the geography of my study dramatically if I could fill the closets with books and files I'm not using at the moment, thereby freeing up bookshelf space I desperately need for dozens of newer books now stacked ignominiously in great piles on the floor. There's even a huge unfinished quilt tucked up in the corner of the closet. I started it years ago as a summer bedspread. Perhaps I can finally finish it, or refashion it into several smaller quilts. In another corner lie all the materials—black fabrics, lining, exquisite laces and ribbons, beads and pearls—for my long envisioned gypsy skirts. When will I ever finally make them?

As I clear old clutter out of my closets and out of my life, what newness am I preparing to welcome in?

July 8th

This morning at breakfast—with two dozen fifteen-page autobiographical essays to be read and graded in short order—I told Steve I imagined living in a large, airy house with a spacious yard and a private patio where we could relax with friends over morning coffee and muffins, with Bach in the background, and the prospect of a beautifully open day ahead. I've had days like that and they are indescribably luxurious. Then a walk around the seawall and a long cold drink in an outdoor restaurant, back home for a shower, and then a barbecue or out for a leisurely dinner. If it could have a European flavor, all the better.

One of the things I miss so much in New York is that seemingly innate European sense of what it means to live graciously and well. That easy sense of delighting in the company of others in the course of a day together. It's so very different from meeting for a rushed dinner in Manhattan or driving for an hour on the infamous

Belt Parkway to meet friends. I often dream of spending time together in a relaxed and beautiful environment where the senses are caressed and we can all ease out of our usual goal-oriented zeal. The film *Enchanted April* perfectly captures the airy, luminous, sensual, joyous atmosphere I yearn for; so does Kenneth Branagh's film version of *Much Ado About Nothing*. Certain music does as well: Canteloube's "Songs of the Auvergne," for example, and Loreena McKennitt's lovely and exotic melodies. For short periods in my life, I have experienced that magical quality. In Florence in the summer of 1979. In Cairo with Heba and her father in 1988. During our summer stays in Vancouver when we meet friends for long relaxing days of sunshine, mellow walks and talks in outdoor cafés, followed by leisurely dinners that last three hours or longer. . . .

Am I a hopeless hedonist? A sensualist, for sure. More likely, I am simply attempting to escape, even if only in fantasy, the reality of all the work facing me before my summer course is over and we fly west at the end of the month!

July 10th

I have been remembering a long conversation in which our sociologist friend Phil asked me which of the three English-speaking countries I've lived in enjoyed the highest standard of living. Wanting to be sure I understood, I asked him whether he did in fact mean standard of living—or quality of life. It seems pretty clear to me that the U.S. has the highest standard of living, but for me, personally, the quality of life was better in both Vancouver and London than it has been in New York City.

There's definitely a subjective element involved here. I suppose it depends on how you measure quality of life. For me, it has to do with access and proximity to family and friends, films, concerts, restaurants, greenmarkets, parks, the mountains, the ocean, and nature in general. Also, with the levels both of pollution and free-floating aggression in the atmosphere, the degree of traffic congestion and road-rage, and the efficiency of public transportation. All of these factors combined seem more important to me than whether cheese and gasoline cost twenty-five percent more or less.

There was an interesting follow-up to that conversation. Not long afterward, Peter Jennings announced on prime time news that, according to a study published in the *Los Angeles Times*, the United Nations had declared Vancouver the best city in the world in which to live, based on more than forty factors such as its cultural life, public education, personal safety, medical care, and much more. So maybe my experience isn't entirely subjective after all, even if they obviously weren't taking annual rainfall into account!

July 11th

I am tired today. I don't know why, since I slept long and well last night. Perhaps it's completing an intense six-week workshop series and the end of my summer autobiographical writing course at the college (with two very busy weeks of reading and grading still ahead), and being anxious about Mum's surgery yesterday, which appears to have gone well. Whatever the reason, I want that perfect vacation I described a few days ago. I want to sit in the shade with a long cool drink, Hermione Lee's new biography of Virginia Woolf, and my journal.

Strange that even with all the space there is in my weekly calendar, I feel burned out and depleted right now. Margery and I often wonder if someone who doesn't take teaching so seriously would feel less exhausted at the end of the term. I do know that to approach a class of thirty or forty students as individuals, each with their own strengths, interests, and desires, takes tremendous energy, which I usually have, and endless patience, which I often lack.

It's especially important in a class like "Autobiographical Writing"—where students naturally share personal information about their lives in their writing—to be sensitive to each person in the class and to help them see what is unique and exceptional in their lives. This is what I love most about teaching, but it's also what leaves me most exhausted. At the end of the three-and-a-half-hour class, I often feel utterly drained, as if someone had pulled me through an old-fashioned wringer washer, all energy squeezed out in the process.

July 12th

I want to have an erotic relationship with the world around me. I'm not talking about sexuality either. That's only one small part of it. I mean that I want to live with all my senses alive and keenly attuned to everything around me; to live fully in my body, even the parts I struggle with, the flabby, droopy, stretch-marked parts. If you are really in your body, inhabiting it all the way from your guts to your skin, then everything you do is charged with sensuality, whether it is taking a walk, sitting in front of the computer, or washing the dishes.

"Erotic" comes from "eros," which surely is not only passionate, romantic love, but the quality of being in love with life itself. I want to repose serenely in my body, gracefully, radiantly, vibrantly—and to give off sparks. Again I'm thrown back to Stephen Nachmanovitch, who writes:

> Eros—the divine principle of desire and love—surges from our deepest evolutionary roots: the urge to create, to generate new life, to regenerate the species. It is the creative energy immanent in us as living beings. . . . Writing, playing, composing, painting; reading, listening, looking—all require that we submit to being swept away by Eros, to a transformation of self of the kind that happens when we fall in love.[43]

I want to vibrate with creative energy. I want to be swept away by Eros.

July 13th

Yesterday I read Elisabeth Kübler-Ross's *The Wheel of Life: A Memoir of Living and Dying.* Her final words of advice are profound:

> It is very important that you do only what you love to do. You may be poor, you may go hungry, you may live in a shabby place, but you will totally live. And at the end of your days, you will bless your life because you have done what you came here to do.[44]

How encouraging to read those words, written by someone who has spent her entire life doing just that, and in the face of every conceivable adversity.

July 16th

Yesterday I did a fruit fast. I made a salad of nectarine, peach, pear, banana, grapes, honeydew melon, and mango in the morning, all organic, and ate it over the course of the day. Late at night my stomach felt very empty, so I ate a small apple. No cooking, cleanup, or dishes to do. I felt light and empty this morning. I should do this every week.

What *would* it be like, I wonder, to live in the country, far enough out so as to have some land with fruit trees, and grow organic vegetables, have a large patio and space for guests, maybe even enough for journal writing retreats? Would we end up feeling isolated, too far removed from good movies and ethnic food? The thought of having plenty of space both in and around our home is so appealing, all the more so if it's near the ocean. If we can get something like that within thirty minutes from Vancouver so that we can go into the city whenever we want, it will be perfect. We could even move to the Sunshine Coast and buy something on the water. That would probably be too far out for me to commute for teaching purposes, however. So many questions about our future, and so many possibilities. More than anything, we just want to be together, but how and where best to integrate Steve's desire to be near the ocean with mine to be near family and friends? I think we'll have great freedom, when we finally relocate, to decide where we really want to live.

July 25th

So much has happened since I last wrote in here. The last of our organic vegetables are in the freezer, ready for the first big pot of autumn soup. I blanched and froze broccoli, red cabbage, celery, red beets, zucchini, mushrooms, green beans, and chives. Nothing will go to waste, and although we have bowed out of the Purple Dragon co-op for now, we'll still be eating organically into September. Preparing that first great pot of soup has become an autumn ritual in which I celebrate the earth's bounty and look ahead to the coming winter. Maybe I'll plan a party for the autumn equinox this year and serve homemade soup and bread.

Last Tuesday Steve went into Brooklyn for the deposition concerning the accident and ten million dollar lawsuit. As we'd hoped, it went well. Our lawyer told Steve, "It's all a scam, and we're not going to pay." Even the other lawyers referred to Steve as the "no-pay." Hopefully this will be the end of this travesty and we'll receive a refund for the unwarranted hike in our insurance rates. It amounts to hundreds of dollars at this point.

And now, I have to pack for our flight to Vancouver tomorrow. Two and a half weeks of relaxing, visiting, walking, and enjoying the company of people I love.

August 11th,
in Chilliwack

Mum and I sorted through several large boxes of fabric last night and cleared out at least twenty pieces, as well as some small remnants and odds and ends. Anna, her Russian friend, will sew children's clothing to send to Russia. We'll probably do this again before long, but at least we've made a start.

As we sorted through one box after another, we were both appalled at the amount of money we have spent on fabrics over the years, some of which have lain there for thirty years and longer; hundreds of dollars' worth, at the time, and probably worth several thousand dollars at today's prices. What did we think would become of all that fabric, I wonder? We found everything from lush velvets and glossy satins to cottons, linens, and wools, even a stack of the indestructible polyesters that went under the label "fortrel" and were all the vogue in the early 1970s. There were fabrics, laces, and exotic trims I'd brought back from Europe, the Middle East, and Mexico, and a gorgeous piece of red silk a friend brought me from Hong Kong. So many memories, and so many grand plans to turn these raw materials into beautiful clothes and decorations.

Throughout my years living at home, Mum and I were passionate about fabric, and we accumulated enough over the years to open our own store. The only problem was that Mum didn't sew much. I sewed up many pieces for her, for Nellie, and myself, and even a few simple dresses for friends, but there was always an enormous backlog; we bought them at a much faster rate than I could sew them. Still, we kept buying more. If I had to guess, I'd say that between us, we still have at least two hundred pieces of varying lengths. Some of them we'll make good use of, I hope. We're hanging on to the cottons and woolens for now. At the very least, I plan to make more quilts and some bathrobes.

I can't help but wonder, though, what hunger were we trying to fill during those years with our compulsive fabric purchases?

August 15th

We are back in New York after an unusually active time in Chilliwack. Because of Mum's back injury when she fell from the hammock, Dad and I were kept much busier than usual with the garden. It was the most sustained and assorted work I have ever done with the summer harvest, all the more miraculous because I hadn't done the planting myself and the sudden plenitude seemed to come out of nowhere. When it comes to gardening, it seems my parents can't do anything wrong. Everything they plant flourishes and the bounty is abundant. We could scarcely keep up.

The first day we made two great pots of applesauce from their apple tree. The prodigious frequency of wormholes testified to the absence of pesticides and made cutting into each apple an adventure; we never knew what we might find! The next day we prepared two pailfuls of string beans for the freezer. Then it was time to pick the cucumbers which were growing at an alarming rate, due to near-perfect conditions of soil and weather. Twelve quarts of dill pickles later, we harvested the basil and made more than a dozen batches of pesto sauce, thick, green, and pungent. Its rich aroma saturated the entire house for the rest of the day.

When Nellie arrived a few days later, we all worked together assembly-line fashion and baked eight large apple cakes and a dozen apple crisps. The organic apples seemed to ripen all at once so we had to work fast. We started early in the day and by mid-afternoon, every bit of counter space was covered with every size and shape of Corningware dish and assorted aluminum baking pans full of rich, buttery apple crisp, ready for the deep freezer.

The whole time Steve and I were in Chilliwack, we feasted on organic vegetables from the garden: carrots, lettuce, Swiss chard, beans, zucchini, potatoes, cucumbers, parsley, dill, and chives. What a healthy delight.

August 25th

I've just returned from a week of teaching "Journal Writing and the Art of Simple Living" for the International Women's Writing Guild's Summer Conference at Skidmore College, and I want to reflect on what happened there. Marion Milner, the British writer and psychoanalyst, describes how, while trying to capture the important highlights of her travels in her diary, she gradually learned to pay attention to the "small private moments that come nuzzling into my thoughts, asking for attention."[45] Milner called them "bead memories" because they contained the essential meaning of the whole event. What are my bead memories of Skidmore this year?

The six-hour dinner I had with Eunice was one of the most provocative and exhilarating conversations I've had in a long time. The discussion skipped and danced, alighting momentarily, then off in a new direction. "Quick-silver," as Kathie and I used to call it; two minds on the same beat, flying. Her relentless energy. Her endless grief over the loss of two beloved partners in seven years. My yearning toward her all week, wanting to comfort but feeling so helpless to do anything but sit and listen.

Lunch with Joan from Texas. Our Marion Woodman lunch, one-on-one, quiet, intense, much intuitive understanding. Her gratitude for the time we shared, and mine.

Looking at Ruth's manuscript on homesteading in the Adirondacks with her, so happy that I could give her helpful feedback.

The woman at dinner, I don't remember her name, who looked at me with such longing as I got up to leave and said, "Please don't go. Can't you stay a little longer?" So I sat down again and we talked. I didn't see her again after that night.

Dancing on the last night. I'd both feared and longed for it all week, and when it finally came I let myself move to the drumbeat, surrendered to the rhythm rising from my body. I felt shameless, ecstatic, a dancing being full of erotic energy. I can hardly describe it. It was glorious.

Bead memories of Skidmore. Most of them quiet. Precious.

But it wasn't all wonderful. My shadow rages at Skidmore. So many workshop directors, some with super-classes. Not that I even want a larger group—my classes ranged from twenty to fifty—but some insecure part of me wants to be "popular" too.

Dare I assume my feelings are not unique? There must be others among the sixty workshop directors who feel overlooked or slighted at times ("I couldn't make it to your workshop, but I wonder if you would look at my manuscript"). In a sense, Skidmore brings out what is both best and worst in me. And the good and the bad are sometimes very close together here in this short week, and magnified, because the entire experience is so intense. Even the piece I wrote in Sandy's class reveals more than I realized at the time I was writing it. She asked us to begin with the words "Now or never," and this is what I wrote:

> August 19th.
>
> Now or never. Fear, fearlessness, speak out, let go, no shame in imperfection. This is where we are right now. Open heart, transparency, bloodflow and pulsing movement, dancing laughter. Don't stop for fear to jump back in; it only comes with second-guessing. So much color, joy, and laughter; so much sorrow, grief, and heartache. Ugliness has its place too. I can only work on my own shadow. You don't get brownie points for taking back projections, but it's so important, for things to be real and substantial. . . .

Then we had to choose one sentence—italicized here—from what we'd written to begin a new paragraph.

> *You don't get brownie points for taking back projections.* No one cares if you understand the root of your own envy, resentment, maliciousness. But *you* care. You *do* care. It means everything to know the tree

is not rotten at its roots, that sturdy green growth springs into reality and vividness, that things really are what they seem.

The world of images is shaky. We are all so sophisticated, so grown-up and self-contained. We are all so vulnerable, so ready for the loving eyes that mirror back the self we've only hoped we could be. Moving in a grown-up world, we are all in masquerade, yearning, hoping against hope that someone will say. . . .

Hoping against hope that someone will say, "Alright. Everybody stop. It's time to take the masks off!"

And if we did that, then what?

Would we stop in awe, shocked that even here, without mask or covering of night, we see ourselves reflected? Would we be ashamed to see the ballroom filled with infants, children, young adults of every age and description? Where would we go from there?

Would we start the music, grab a partner, swing and sway, and dance to the rhythm leaping from the body? Feel free to start all over again? What it if came out differently the next time around?

Transparency. No need for second-guessing. No need to make or wear the mask that hides the face that wants and does not want to be known. Just a shared breath, a whispered affirmation.

I don't know where that came from, but as soon as I'd written it I knew it was true—and very revealing. How difficult it can be to get past the careful generalizations of academic discourse to the spontaneous rhythms of the hearts, in writing. My brain unbidden overlays my heart's experience with a layer of rational analysis. Even here, in this journal.

August 26th

The refrigerator is full after our big shopping trip yesterday afternoon and the freezer is stuffed to the limit with eight large loaves of Mum's bread that we brought back with us. Over the next few days I want to cook ahead for the semester, especially since we'll have Nellie and family here for ten days in October. I'd like to have most of our meals worked out in advance so we don't have to spend too much time in the kitchen. If we keep things simple it should be fine. Muffins and muesli in the morning, sandwiches at lunch, and lots of fruit.

Yesterday's post brought a letter from our insurance broker informing us that the claims adjustor has finally decided we have no liability whatsoever in the accident and shouldn't be penalized. Our premiums will return to normal and we'll receive a refund for the extra we have already paid. Thrilled, I immediately rang Steve at his office and gave him the good news. Maybe this is the beginning of the end of this minor nightmare and the unnecessary anxiety and fragmentation it has brought into our lives.

Meanwhile, it's almost a week since I returned from Skidmore, but I still haven't really found my beat. I'm restless and can't quiet down internally, not enough to work the way I want to, anyway. While at Skidmore, I met Randy Rolfe, a great-niece of Scott and Helen Nearing. Randy told me that Helen died in a car accident recently at the age of 91. One miserably wet night she got it into her head to go into town to see a film and wouldn't be talked out of it. On the drive in, her car hit a slippery patch and went off the road. How ironic that someone who spent her entire life in the most healthful way possible should end up dying an unnatural death. I wonder if some part of her simply felt she'd lived long enough and was ready to move on.

August 29th

During the Persian Gulf War in 1991 I began to make patchwork quilts. For hours each evening as we watched CNN's live coverage of the latest horrors, I cut out hundreds of three- and six-inch squares of calico cottons in all colors of the rainbow, exulting in the beauty of the floral prints and the texture of the fabric in my hands. I did this for weeks. Much later, when I described it to my friend Gabi in England, she told me she'd taken up knitting during the same period, and several friends of hers in London had also begun hands-on creative projects. Gabi had a theory that we were all subconsciously trying to counter the destruction and horror of the war by creating something beautiful that would delight and nurture another human being.

It was a cold winter. I remember sitting at the dining room table and snipping away as the piles of squares grew higher and higher. I remember the visceral enjoyment of arranging them on our bed in order to get a pleasing harmony of darker and lighter colors in the quilt face. The war ended, and I continued to sew four-squares into eight-squares and eight-squares into blocks of sixteen. Beautiful to look at and so perfect for snuggling on a chilly winter day, I made five quilts for my family that winter. My nephew, almost a teenager now, still sleeps under those electric red, blue, and yellow dinosaurs grinning idiotically on their black background.

I know I can't prevent war. I can't even protect those I love most from pain or suffering. But I can care for them, make sure they know in their bones how much they are loved. We do what we can.

August 31st

I'm still reflecting on my week at Skidmore. My experience there is anything but simple; every emotion feels larger than life. Such a complex whirl of exultation and inadequacy, of self-affirmation and self-doubt, of ego reinforcement and bruising. What an intense week of community with other women who write and share many of my passions and beliefs. Of course I bask in the warmth of other women's affirmation of my book and journal class. All through the year I do my best to offer encouragement and support to my students, and then in the course of that one week in August, I receive more positive feedback than I do throughout the rest of the year (someone even told me that I had the most beautiful earrings at the Conference). "You have such a lovely energy," I heard. And, "You are the best listener I have ever met, bar none." That comment touched me more than any other.

I do believe that part of simple living is giving each moment and each person the courtesy of my full and undivided attention. I try to put my own preoccupations aside and clear a space in which I can really see and take them into myself, enter their inner world to feel something of what they are feeling. Sometimes I succeed. Too often, I fall short. But I keep trying, because I know what it's like when someone gives me the gift of their whole attention, how cherished and energized I feel afterward. There's nothing more powerful than that kind of listening, that experience of being seen and heard for who we truly are.

September 1st

Decades before the folks who "learned it all at kindergarten," Helen and Scott Nearing offered a wonderfully concise summary of "tips on de-stressing one's life."[46] Here it is, making me smile at the no-nonsense wisdom it contains, even for those of us who shudder at the thought of an earthworm touching our well-manicured hands.

1. Do the best you can, whatever arises
2. Be at peace with yourself
3. Find a job you enjoy

4. Live in simple conditions: housing, food, clothing; get rid of clutter
5. Contact nature every day; feel the earth under your feet
6. Take physical exercise through hard work; through gardening or walking
7. Don't worry; live one day at a time
8. Share something every day with someone else; if you live alone, write someone; give something away; help someone else somehow
9. Take time to wonder at life and the world; see some humor in life where you can
10. Observe the one life in all things
11. Be kind to the creatures

Stated with beautiful simplicity, it seems to me that this just about says it all.

September 3rd

This morning I received a call from a local women's organization. They want me to be part of a panel on "women trying to have it all." The problem is that the event takes place in less than two weeks. And there was no mention of any honorarium or payment, even though I know they routinely pay guest speakers.

"You would only have to speak for about ten minutes," the caller said. "I know it's very short notice, but we would sure like to have you."

"I'm sorry," I told her. "It's not enough lead time. I teach three nights a week and I need a little more notice than that." I also need to be paid for my time and expertise, but I didn't say that. I have been so reluctant to raise the issue of payment when people ask me to speak. "It's only ten minutes." "It's for a women's group. Women's groups never have much money." "It's for a good cause." "You can sell your book, and you'll get new people for your mailing list." There's a dozen reasons to do it for free. I know them all and have done many talks and seminars for worthy causes without remuneration.

Only, I don't want to do that anymore. I have known for quite some time now that giving endless lectures and workshops for free is not smart. Then I discussed it with Louise, a feisty and successful business woman at Skidmore. She said people don't value what they get for free and if they really want you, they'll come back with an offer of payment and increased respect to boot. She said the only thing I should be doing for free is what I volunteer to do, never because someone requests it. She was absolutely clear and adamant that I should not offer my professional expertise without financial remuneration—especially since most often it's for people earning much more money than I do. I listened with fascination. I suspected as much, but it was important to hear her say it.

This is the second time this group has asked me to step in at short notice and do a presentation for them, with no mention of payment. Where is the respect for my professional services in this? If they want me to address them, why don't they send me an official invitation along with an offer of payment? This time I was very clear. I simply said "no."

Along similar lines, several days ago I received a request in the mail from a freelance writer doing an article on journal writing. She had been told by a woman who attended one of my workshops that I've written a book on women's journals, so she sent me a very basic two-page questionnaire ("When and why did you begin keeping a journal?") and requested that I, "as an expert," complete it and return it ASAP. No attempt to acquaint herself with my work, not even a self-addressed stamped envelope, the most basic professional courtesy.

I considered sending her a postcard suggesting she read my book for the answers to her questions, but decided just to toss the questionnaire out. It seemed the right thing to do. I can't imagine acting that presumptuously toward someone from whom I hoped to get information for an article. I think that I'm finally realizing that I don't have to say "yes" to everyone who asks me for something. It's *my time* and *my life energy* at stake, and people who act as if they have a claim on it don't warrant the courtesy of a postmarked "no." Perhaps deciding not to entertain inappropriate requests is also a way to simplify my life.

September 15th

As I cooked and ate chicken the other day, I was not enjoying it. I hate handling raw meat of any kind, which is unavoidable in washing and skinning it. I could probably be a moderate vegetarian, eating only eggs and cheese, if only Steve could tolerate beans and lentils better. His digestive tract rebels so strongly that at most I use them sparingly in soups and pasta sauces.

On a rational level, I can be convinced that it is not a good thing to slaughter living creatures for food. All the more so when they were bred solely for that purpose and have led miserable lives only to be prematurely butchered. And I believe the reports about how unhealthy meat is for human consumption, and how much antibiotic and other dangerous drugs are routinely pumped into the animals and end up in our poor beleaguered bodies.

Even so, I cannot quite convince myself to give it up. I am convinced we can, should, and will eat less meat, and by meat, I really mean chicken. We don't eat pork, lamb, or veal, and only very rarely a little beef. I can even see going without chicken for a week or two, but for the rest of my life? I guess the answer is in the twelve-step program's advice to take it one day at a time. But I'm not prepared to go "cold turkey" just yet.

Still, the distaste I have always felt while handling raw animal flesh seems to be growing, and I wouldn't be surprised if I do swear off it entirely one day. Only, to be consistent, I suppose I'd have to give up leather handbags as well. That would be more difficult for me. Meanwhile, as a halfway measure, I may cut down on our use of poultry or possibly even stop cooking chicken altogether. If we crave it, we can always order it in a restaurant.

September 22nd

A gorgeous crisp morning on this first day of autumn. It feels good to be back in this journal after too much time away these past few months.

I felt downhearted last week, even somewhat depressed. I couldn't think of anything that I wanted to do, anything that seemed important. Yesterday I had a busy day of cooking. Perhaps that was therapeutic, because now I feel better. I made a large pot of soup for the week, two dozen corn muffins, a carrot-pineapple cake for Wednesday's workshop, some carrot muffins, and a pot of applesauce. I hadn't had a domestic day like that in a long time, so it was a nice change. I imagine that body and soul needed that rhythm, those particular gestures.

About three weeks ago I began to jog again. I haven't jogged in six or seven years—can't recall why I stopped—but it's amazing how quickly the body remembers. I thought it would take me months to build up my capacity, but I've already jogged a continuous four miles, albeit slowly. The goal I have set for myself is eventually to run five or six miles in an hour, four to five times a week. I managed four runs last week.

It pleases me to think of myself as a jogger. It's so at odds with my decades-long unkind perception of myself as a klutz and lazy slug when it came to physical activity, because the only exercise I did happily was a lot of walking. There's such a wonderful sense of freedom running on the boardwalk with the ocean on one side and clear blue skies above. Today, especially, it was a joy. Sixty-five degrees out, and brilliantly clear. I started slowly, with various aches and pains and not much energy. But I gained momentum as I ran, and ended up running five miles in my best time yet. I'll be joining the New York marathon before long at this rate!

September 23rd

Opa Schiwy, my last remaining grandparent, died yesterday, just three months before his 101st birthday. When we saw him in August he was well and happy, and had begun to gain back some of the weight he'd lost during his recent hospitalization. I thought for sure we'd have another birthday celebration in December. But my uncle came home after work last night to find Opa gone, lying on his bed with his glasses on, looking very peaceful. Perhaps he drifted away in the course of lying down to nap. I'd like to think it was in the middle of a good dream.

I didn't feel great sadness or loss, although I loved him dearly. He'd told Dad he didn't care to live through another winter, but at last report, he was doing so well that this news was unexpected, in as far as death at the age of one hundred years can come as a surprise. The funeral is next Monday, but I will not fly home to be there. Having seen him very much alive only five weeks ago, I have no need to say goodbye to his body.

Opa had a very difficult life. He was conscripted to fight in both world wars and suffered enormously. Only three of his eight children survived childhood, and when he was finally able to bring his family to Canada after the war, they lived in poverty for years. Honest, hard-working, and unpretentious, Opa's faith in God sustained him through many hardships and losses. I never heard him complain. Quiet, reserved, and undemonstrative, I was surprised when I went to say goodbye before leaving for England to see tears in his eyes after he hugged me. As I walked down the driveway I said, "I love you, Opa," and he called out to me in his accented English, "I love you too," the only words he ever spoke to me in English.

Perhaps he simply couldn't say them in German, but I knew that in his quiet way, he loved all seven of his grandchildren.

I'm so happy that I have the beautiful mahogany bookcase he made for me and the black and red velvet cushion that Oma sewed so many years ago. Nellie, Irma, and Angela have quilts that Oma made, so we all have their concrete presences in our homes. Goodbye, dear Opa.

September 25th

So often, my mental process is anything but simple. I want it to be quiet, clear, unsullied by complicated twists and turns. Then a hundred mitigating factors arise: "Yes but," and "what if," and "if only," and "on the other hand." Inner and outer again. How can there be simplicity when the mind is filled with convoluted knots of anxiety and nervous tension?

Maybe we can never get rid of those mental knots. Maybe the best we can do is make them more conscious and observe them, thereby lessening their destructive energy. Maybe one of the goals of simple living, like that of psychoanalysis, is to bring the invisible to light (it takes great energy to keep blinding oneself to the truth). Maybe I'm too curmudgeonly today to have anything inspiring or uplifting to say about simplicity. I just can't make myself rise above it all or pretend that fragmentation is only an illusion. I am hungry for reality, for what is real in this very tangible, visceral, fleshy world I inhabit.

Pamela came to the workshop last night, even though she was still in pain and exhausted by her second lumpectomy last Friday. How devastating it must have been to discover—through a lucky fluke—another lump in her breast, after seven months of chemotherapy and the loss of her beautiful, curly, long black hair. She looked haunted. Again I felt the terrible helplessness of wanting to do something and knowing there's so little I or anyone else can do for her, despite our love and concern.

I am also concerned about Barbara. Last Wednesday she said that her goal at the beginning of this workshop series was to find meaning in her life. I think she means something exalted and spiritual. But meanwhile, her physical health is not good. She just turned sixty, tells me she doesn't exercise or eat wisely, and feels unwell much of the time. As she spoke, I thought that perhaps the "meaning in life" she is looking for lies in tending to her physical body, "caring for her beloved animal," as Marion Woodman would say, nurturing and strengthening it as much as possible. The fact that she is getting back to her singing may be a good sign. What I find so endearing about Barbara is that her emotions are so close to the surface. She is expansive, enthusiastic, always ready to be moved and delighted. Such a large and generous spirit. But I think she needs to care for her bodily home now. Perhaps I could mention this to her. It might be something she hasn't thought of herself.

October 2nd

As this journal on simple living draws to a close, I feel that I ought to have made some earth-shaking discovery in the past twelve months, to have unearthed some profound truth about living simply that will take me into the next year and the next century and millennium. Yet there has been no dramatic turning point, no great flash of insight that changed my life, and no major change in our living circumstances.

Meanwhile this is the calm before the storm. In ten days, Nellie and family arrive and the house will be filled with activity for a week and a half. It will be good to spend such a long stretch of time with my twelve-year-old nephew and ten-year-old niece. We have never had more than a weekend with Stefan and Chelsea before. Until their arrival I want to write, to give the house a long-postponed cleaning and clear out my study so that they can use it as a storage room for suitcases and clothes, to bake chocolate chip cookies, and to enjoy the quiet rhythm of our days together.

Here is my favorite all-purpose chocolate chip cookie recipe, an adaptation of a recipe given to me by Laurence in London, more than a decade ago.

Crunchy Chocolate Chip Cookies

1 cup butter, softened
1 cup packed dark brown sugar
2/3 cup sugar
2 eggs
2 tsp. vanilla
3 cups whole wheat flour
1 cup oats, either quick-cooking or whole oats put through the blender
1 tsp. baking powder
1 tsp. salt
1 to 2 cups chocolate chips
* 1/2 cup coconut, flaked or desiccated
* 1/2 cup sunflower seeds or chopped nuts
* 1 cup raisins

*The last three ingredients are optional but add flavor and crunchiness.

Cream butter and sugars lightly with wooden spoon. Add eggs and vanilla. Mix all remaining ingredients together and combine with wet ingredients. Mix with hands for best results and don't overmix. Drop large tablespoons onto greased baking sheet and flatten with a fork into a round shape. Bake at 375° F for 15 minutes. This makes 25-30 large crunchy cookies.

October 4th

I spent several hours yesterday clearing out paper in my study. Only now am I emotionally able to throw out the many drafts of my first book, including those with Steve's and my editor's comments. I suppose the whole process of writing *A Voice of Her Own* was so important to me that I didn't want to part with any of it. But yesterday I finally made a beginning. Is it significant, I wonder, that this occurred on my forty-fourth birthday? I'd resolved to spend the day doing only what I wanted to, and I ended up going for a run, working on my study, baking cookies, and then Steve and I went to Taste of India for dinner.

I threw out materials related to my dissertation, most of our wedding cards, the last few years' Christmas cards, drafts of articles I've written over the years, reprints of articles from other people, and all our bills and statements from before 1994. I also junked thirty or forty job applications from the early '90s. I'd forgotten just how much effort I'd put into looking for a position during those early years in New York. At that time I'd have been thrilled with the job offer I had last year. That was before I started the Women's Journal Workshop and decided to write the journal book.

But there's a lot still to sort through. In the closet sit two boxes of Christa Wolf material, all related to my doctoral work. I'm quite sure I'll never look at any of it again. There's a whole afternoon's worth of work right there, just deciding how much to throw out. And of course there are my clothes to sort through once more, as well. Yesterday I tried on the Liberty shirt I wore the night Steve and I met, twelve years ago. It fit me for the first time in years, and so I wore it to my birthday dinner tonight at Lundy's Restaurant in Sheepshead Bay. Though he's usually not very sentimental, Steve liked the idea.

October 8th

Barbara called to thank me for the message I left on her answering machine last week. I'd told her what I had been thinking about: that perhaps the spiritual meaning of her life right now is to take loving care of her body and nurture herself as much as possible in every way. She thanked me for my kindness in thinking of her and said she had been turning it over in her mind and would be making it the focus of her reflections on Yom Kippur this Saturday. Whether or not my words actually contain any profound truth is beside the point, I think. What she appreciated was that I'd been thinking of her and took the time to tell her so. It moves me that people are so appreciative of simple gestures of concern like a telephone call asking, "Have you thought of this?" But I am too. We are all so busy that it doesn't happen often enough.

And—speaking of Yom Kippur, the day of atonement and forgiveness—could this be the occasion for trying to make peace with Claudia in my heart of hearts? I still perseverate on our conflicts too much and would like to reach some sort of lasting peace within myself about it. I may have to accept the fact that we really are like oil and water to each other, but I want to be at peace.

October 10th

The house is cleaner than it has been for some time, and it's a delightful feeling. The new shower curtain is up, my study is ready for our visitors, and this afternoon we'll do a big grocery shop to stock up on staples. At 9:20 p.m. tomorrow, my sister and family arrive at JFK Airport. It will be interesting to see what Stefan and Chelsea think of New York.

The other day, I heard Elisabeth Kübler-Ross telling Oprah Winfrey that the only people who speak the truth anymore are psychotics, very young children, and the dying. Everybody else is too busy trying to live up to an image. I wonder if she is right.

October 21st

The Brandts have come and gone. We had a wonderful time together. Steve and I agree that it could not have gone any better than it did. They were appreciative of every least bit of effort and so helpful and independent in every way, that I felt we had all the blessing of visitors without any of the stresses. And I think they were comfortable here, too. The wide open dining-living room area was a perfect space to spend time together without tripping over each other.

For Canadian Thanksgiving we made a big roast turkey dinner with baked potatoes and squash stuffed with apples and cinnamon. I'd have liked a little more time just to relax and talk and maybe even sing together, and it would have been nice to walk or run on the boardwalk more often (we only managed it once). But it sounds as if they'll come again before we move. It seemed luxurious to have family around for so long. Now the house is quiet and it will take a day or two for me to adjust and not set six places at mealtimes. I'm giving myself today for decompression after the busy weekend and class last night.

One thing I did not do much of during their visit is write in my journal, and I know that there's unexplored experience waiting to be reflected on in the days and weeks to come. I share May Sarton's sentiment, expressed here: "I feel cluttered when there is no time to analyze experience. That is the silt—unexplored experience that literally chokes the mind."[47] It amazes me to think that some people never take the time to reflect on their experience, to clear out the silt. Doesn't it eventually build up and clog the soul and psyche? No wonder people do such stupid things at times, without even understanding why.

I do love New York in the autumn. There is so much brilliant sunlight. The colors are glorious, and the temperature perfect. It is cold, crisp, clear, and exhilarating. I hope it lasts.

October 22nd

I made a "Lost Nation Apple Cake" for my workshop tonight. It tastes wonderful: rich, buttery, full of New Paltz apples, with a brown sugar and walnut crumb topping.

Our annual apple-picking trip up to New Paltz, a hundred miles north of the City, has become one of my favorite rituals of autumn in New York. It's a Thanksgiving in itself, especially with family here, for the first time ever, to share my enjoyment. Despite the cloudy weather that day, as we drove farther and farther north on the Palisades Parkway, the colors became more vivid and the foliage was quite beautiful. We had our usual lunch at the Gay Nineties Bistro, then went straight to Apple Hill Farm along Route 32, for the winter's supply of apples and squash. We got fewer apples than last year: probably about seventy-five pounds of Cortland, Empire, Golden Delicious, and several other types. We also picked up about fifteen squash: butternut, acorn, buttercup, spaghetti, and a beautiful orange and dark green variety I haven't seen before. Nellie took pictures of us all sitting on a tractor, surrounded by pumpkins, and then, the car trunk full of bounty, we drove back into town to poke through the bookstores and other little shops. We ended up at Barnaby's for a light early supper and shared a piece of their wicked chocolate peanut pie before driving back to Staten Island in heavy rain. Nellie, Stefan, and I promptly set about turning the utility grade Golden Delicious apples into applesauce. It is the most delicious batch ever, and beautiful, too, because of its golden hue. Yesterday I made two dozen whole wheat applesauce muffins, and all the remaining apples are now safely in the refrigerator.

This weekend I'll make Steve's favorite apple recipe—Mum's German-style apple cake. Here it is.

Lilli's Apfelkuchen (two cakes)

5 cups unbleached all-purpose flour (I substitute up to 2 cups of whole wheat flour)
1 1/2 cups sugar
3-4 eggs
2 rounded tablespoons baking powder
2 tsp. vanilla or lemon rind
1 1/2 cups butter or margarine, softened
1/2 tsp. salt
2 pounds of apples, peeled, cored, and thickly sliced, any variety that isn't mealy

Measure and mix sifted flour, baking powder, salt, and sugar in a large mixing bowl. Beat together eggs, vanilla or lemon rind, and softened butter or margarine. Add to flour mixture and knead with your hands, until thoroughly blended. Then press into two medium-sized cake pans, either with a rolling pin or with the palm of your hand. Cover with thickly sliced apples. Bake at 350° F, for about 30 minutes, until golden. When it has cooled off a little, sprinkle with a mixture of 1/4 cup sugar and 1 tsp. cinnamon. This apple cake is lovely for breakfast or brunch. As dessert, serve it warm with a scoop of vanilla ice cream or a dollop of whipped cream.

October 23rd

Simplicity.
Simple living.
Every day, appreciating how much I have in life.

Noticing how much beauty there is in the world.
Refusing to take things for granted.
Acknowledging the gratitude I so often feel.
Getting off automatic pilot and directing my own course.
All my senses alive to the world.

October 24th

In the late autumn and winter I am not in the mood to teach. I want to stay in and write, have coffee klatches with my friends, listen to "Secret Garden," and dream in my journal. There's definitely a psychic rhythm to the seasons, which is why I could not live in a place like Florida where it's summer all year around, or in the far north, where it is dark and frozen seven or eight months of the year. As the weather gets colder and the nights grow longer, I feel the urge to nestle in for the winter, make apple crumble, and start another patchwork quilt. I don't feel the same urge to be out in the world as I do in the summer. The nesting instinct kicks in and I want to be warm and cozy on the living room couch in my big cherry red cardigan, with a pot of apple cinnamon tea and a good book. Never mind that the bulk of the term's marking load is still ahead of me!

This year, Christmas shopping should not be a problem. We drew names among the adults which will mean less head-scratching there. Nellie will shop for Mum and I'll get Dad's gift. Not that I don't enjoy buying gifts for them both, but since there seems to be little that they need or want, we are often at a loss. I've already discussed cutting back on gift exchanges with friends as well, and in some cases we're stopping altogether. I estimate that I've cut back by fifty percent this year, and I'm delighted with progress made in this area of my attempt to simplify.

Last night I went into the City to hear Wanda Urbanska, co-author of *Simple Living,* give a talk at the New School. She was lovely. Clear, direct, and warm. When a member of the audience asked how this simple living lifestyle works for single people, she said that it involves finding security in relationships and community rather than in money or possessions. I wondered how some of the sophisticated New Yorkers in the audience reacted to her answer. It seems to me that there's a lot of truth to what she said, but I haven't found an abundance of that sort of friendship in New York. I suspect it's rare anywhere in large urban settings.

October 25th

As my yearlong journal of simple living draws to a close, where has this quiet inner journey brought me? To be sure, I haven't quit my job and moved to a small town, gotten rid of the car, or become a vegetarian. Nor have there been other major upheavals in my life. But I do have a clear sense that things have changed. Subtly, but irrevocably, in many areas of my life from household routines and long-range financial goals to my understanding of friendship and discerning use of time.

To begin with, I have cleared three enormous garbage bags of paper and assorted clutter from my study, including stacks of greeting cards and letters, almost a decade's worth of old bills, statements, and job applications, and numerous drafts of my first book. I have given away or thrown out a quarter of my wardrobe (with again as much still to go), in the process reclaiming items of clothing that I haven't worn in years. The next step will be to sort through my books, both my personal library and my teaching materials, to determine what is worth shipping to Vancouver. This is not a prospect I contemplate with equanimity; I have a hard time even throwing out old magazines.

As far as our household routines are concerned, we seem to have found a rhythm that suits us. Every six or eight weeks we load up the car with staple items from the supermarket, then pick up what we need between times at the local grocery and farmer's market. I'm becoming expert at cooking in huge quantities as our stuffed freezer will attest, stacked to the brim with ready-to-go suppers for the rest of the term. My cooking routine has grown simpler all around: I rarely cook more than once or twice a week, yet we always eat well. Our cleaning chores remain minimal.

In the area of health and personal concerns, I've altered my exercise routine to suit my current circumstances. Frustrated and discouraged by the lack of visible results after a year and a half of regular visits to the gym, I stopped going. After a seven-year hiatus—I'm not quite sure why I stopped—I have happily resumed jogging once more. Not coincidentally, I've lost more than twenty pounds over the course of the year. And at a time when most North Americans suffer from chronic sleep deprivation, I have hardly used the alarm clock at all this past year; what a luxury in this day and age. My wardrobe has also undergone changes (who'd have thought one could live so well in pants?), and I have all but stopped wearing pantyhose and makeup. This has saved me time, money, and plenty of aggravation over stockings that tear the first time I put them on.

On the emotional front, I have laid several difficult relationships to rest, with a sense of sadness, to be sure, but not of personal failure. I have also been trying to pay close attention to my communication with others. It's not always easy to distinguish between speaking truthfully and being overly blunt; between striving for greater intimacy and encroaching on another's comfort zone. But I do believe it is worth the effort if we don't want to remain at arm's length from each other forever.

Our financial prospects continue to become clearer to me. Since Steve will soon be taking early retirement and his pension will not be adjusted for inflation, I have started a small tax-sheltered retirement fund. When it kicks in fifteen years hence, my pension should give us the margin of comfort we'll need by then. Meanwhile, as the time grows near, we are feeling confident that we'll be able to live comfortably enough in Vancouver on his pension and my anticipated part-time income.

For the past year, I have tracked every dollar spent and now have a much better understanding of where my money goes: a considerable sum on eating out, to my surprise, and, less surprisingly, on airfare to Vancouver. (Many restaurant meals, it turns out, serve as the means of maintaining social ties. It seems New Yorkers prefer to conduct their friendships in public spaces rather than invite people into their homes. Even some of my close friends do this, and with time I have reluctantly followed suit. I suppose I could have continued inviting people in for dinner, but I'm bothered by one-sided hospitality, over the long term. I think it needs an element of mutuality to be authentic.) I have found Dominguez and Robin's concept of money as concrete units of life-energy useful in deciding how casually I want to fling my hard-earned cash around, and I know that I've made small but significant changes in my spending in the course of the year.

Wherever possible, I've put a halt to junk mail, unnecessary subscriptions and memberships, and obligatory social engagements. I've cut down drastically on ritual gift-giving as well, and am offering homemade carrot cake or pesto sauce rather than yet another pair of earrings or a bottle of bubble bath. Better yet, I prefer to invite a friend for a birthday lunch and let the time together be a gift to both of us.

I've streamlined teaching preparation and essay grading without compromising my academic standards. After a decade of teaching college writing, I've realized, it really isn't necessary to spend hours preparing for class. Since I know the course material so well, my teaching is actually fresher and more spontaneous if I haven't rehearsed it in detail just before class. It seems to be working well.

And in all things great and small, I have become a more conscious consumer. Whether it is groceries, office supplies, or personal indulgences, I can more readily distinguish *needs* from *wants* and make decisions accordingly. I haven't felt at all inclined to buy or accumulate things, either. Right now my mantra is: If I don't buy it, I won't have to move it three thousand miles. For the first time since my school days in Chilliwack, I have made good use of the public library as well, grateful that they could even obtain, through interlibrary loans, books no longer in print.

And finally, there is the ever-fascinating issue of time. What is it for, and will I ever have enough? On occasions when I feel pressure to do everything at once, it seems to be easier now to step back, breathe deeply, and begin to get an overall felt sense of what is most important to me at that moment. I'm more readily saying no to things I really don't want to do. Even workshops. At times when I feel the need to justify my existence through unrelenting productivity, I remind myself of a favorite passage in May Sarton's *Journal of a Solitude*, where she reflects,

> I always forget how important the empty days are, how important it may be sometimes not to expect to produce anything, even a few lines in a journal. . . . A day where one has not pushed oneself to the limit seems a damaged damaging day, a sinful day. Not so! The most valuable thing we can do for the psyche, occasionally, is to let it rest, wander, live in the changing light of a room, not try to be or do anything whatever.[48]

What has become more clear to me than ever in the course of this year is that it's not the occasional grand splash of "big things"—prestige, material luxury, exotic travel—that gives me a sense of richness and meaning from one day to the next and makes it worth my while to get up in the morning. It's the unending stream of small comforts that nourishes and sustains me: my leisurely morning journal entry, a good cup of coffee with a friend at Edgar's Café in New York or Calhoun's in Vancouver, an hour of singing in the middle of the afternoon, teaching a lively and stimulating class, offering or receiving a word of appreciation, jogging by the Atlantic in the late afternoon, a long distance chat with Mum, dinner and a good movie in Manhattan with Steve on a Sunday night.

I want always to celebrate the simple joys we so often take for granted: healthy bodies and a good night's rest; a walk by the ocean with one's beloved or an afternoon café latté with a cherished friend; the smell of fresh-baked muffins and autumn in the air; a quiet evening of journal writing and listening to music by candlelight. Christa Wolf referred to this as "the precious everyday"; Sue Bender, as the "everyday sacred." These are the pearls of rich contentment in my life.

October 27th

As the jogging begins to bear results, I am getting pleasure from reclaiming clothes I haven't worn in a long time. The smart, long-sleeved black top I wore to class last night fits beautifully now, as it was always meant to but never before did. Now that I fit into those newly-rediscovered items of clothing, I have enough to last me for some time. I am glad I didn't give everything away because some of it I really like and it will serve a purpose in my simplified, smaller-size wardrobe. I have other new items that I haven't even worn and that ought to fit these days too. A black skirt. A red skirt. I probably don't even have to buy very much.

My fit, streamlined self.

Yes. I *am* proud of myself for persevering. I'm feeling more and more myself as my shape takes on more definition, still rounded but less puffy. Much more my true form. By spring I ought to be happily settled into that streamlined self. Then I can think about what I might need in my wardrobe, a few basic items like a black jacket or suit, perhaps a black corduroy jumper again, at long last, and so on. Meanwhile, how nice that I don't have to rush out to shop for new things. I have enough for now. I'm especially pleased that several wool sweaters I purchased in London more than ten years ago and have worn steadily over the years are still serviceable. So much changes when clothes are valued for comfort and quality rather than as a measure of self-esteem or a signal of fashion know-how.

How much of my interest in domesticity—cooking, baking, sewing, budgeting—has to do with wanting to "get back to basics," I wonder? Wanting to clear away clutter of all kinds. Wanting a warm and comfortable home, love and affection, independence and time to nourish my soul, music and books, laughter and fresh air, healthy food and exercise. These are the basics, the necessities, the essentials for me. These are what make up the good life.

In the age of ulcers, chronic fatigue syndrome, and other stress-related illnesses, I have had one cold in the past six years. While many around me are subject to grueling work weeks with frequent mandatory overtime, I enjoy time to write, sing, cook and bake from scratch, sew, conduct workshops and book groups for women, exercise regularly, and travel several times a year. I have been able to invent a life that suits me very well, a life of tremendous creative freedom. For this I count myself so very fortunate.

I am forty-four years old now. Even if I live to a ripe old age, this is roughly the halfway point in my life. As I was jogging today, I thought that I want to regard each day as a gift to be savored. I want to live consciously and alertly; to make every day count and find joy and happiness in it. I don't want to miss any of it through unconsciousness.

October 31st

At the beginning of my year of simple living I said I wanted to see, in true and vivid colors, what matters most to me. Indeed, this was more than a metaphor because from the time I was young I have always experienced everything from numbers to musical composers in terms of *colors*. As the seasons come full circle now, I see that certain colors in the palette of my life have grown more vivid and distinct, while others have faded gently into the background.

The rich deep burgundy and plum of my journal writing and women's writing circle continue to grow more intense. The very idea of a women's journal workshop is something of a paradox, since journal writing is such an intimate affair. And yet, over and over, women tell me that in the comfort and safety of the group, they find courage to face issues they've never before been able to consider, much less commit to paper. I think the experience of writing in silent communion with others is rare and precious, and increases the potential for self-knowledge, creativity, and empowerment.

The radiant dark blue of the love I share with Steve remains the unfailing background and precious constant on the canvas of my life, a steady presence that I never take for granted. The other constant is the lush forest green of my writing, which has always been the core of my life and will accompany me, I trust, through the rest of my years. The paler green of my teaching is much more variable, ranging from a sea-green at the best of times, when a human connection is palpable and the excitement of intellectual inquiry crackles in the classroom, to a murkier hue when I'm beset by oversized writing classes and inadequately prepared and immature students. Personal relationships, too, vary in intensity from the delicate pale pink of a promising first encounter to the rich ruby radiance of a tried and tested friendship that will not easily dim. I'm still exploring the infinite range of shades in between; they deepen and fade as time and inclination allow.

Walking and jogging cast a vibrant turquoise hue, full of air and sky and water, reminding me that every cell in my body pulses with energy. And at last the dusky velvet rose of my singing is beginning to glow again. I am, oh joy, finding my way back into music, as if awakening from a long unplanned and unwelcome slumber, and celebrating how much vibrant color that adds to my life.

Still I long for more of the mauve and goldenrod of travel near and far; the soft eggshell blue of a child in my life; the burnt orange and sienna tones of dance; the pulsating purple of meaningful intellectual challenge; the clear pure yellow of spontaneous joy, and the burnished gold of creativity. Everything in its time.

Paradoxically, what this year has shown me is that to live simply—with integrity, unblinking vision, and a harmony of intention—is far from an easy task. In a world filled with complex alternatives, it demands a barometric sensitivity to our own changing priorities, a constant vigilance against the seductions of productivity and importance, and a willingness to leave behind much that may be important but is not essential, to revive Helen Luke's distinction.

I think, too, that simple living involves a recognition of limits. It means accepting, both once and for all and every day anew, that in my lifetime and in yours, we will not be or do everything we had hoped. I will never be a concert soprano, for example, nor a physician or Jungian analyst, a mother of six, or perhaps even a mother at all. I'll never live in exotic world capitals or speak eight languages, just as surely as I'll never be three inches taller or have red hair. But it is within the growing recognition and acceptance of who and what we truly are, I believe, that we are finally free to celebrate the fullness of our existence and to take our place in the never-ending dance of life.

Rilke's advice, *"Live* the questions now," continues to resonate; I often thought while writing that this book should be titled *A Journal of Questions.* And the steady focus on "what matters most?" will, I believe, allow us to "live along some distant day into the answer," an answer that will never be static or final, but will always reflect the fluid rhythms of our lives. Things and circumstances change. People change. But I do know, by faith and by the experience that this year has brought to me, that there *are* answers to be lived along the way.

Epilogue

. . . Tell me, what is it you plan to do
with your one wild and precious life?

—Mary Oliver, "The Summer Day"

Earlier this year Steve and I made our long-anticipated millennial move to Vancouver, Canada. After almost two decades of longing for the jagged snow-covered mountains and mercurial skies of the Pacific Northwest, I have finally come home.

In our cozy ground-floor apartment on the University Endowment Lands, I am close to much that was dear to me when I left Vancouver on my thirtieth birthday, seventeen years ago: the stunning panorama of ocean and many-layered mountains, abundant walking trails, bookstores, concerts, alternative cinema, ethnic restaurants and cafés. And, of course, to my family and friends.

The picture window in our spacious living room looks out on manicured grass, shrubs, and flowers, beyond which lies an open park like an English green, where students and university employees eat their lunch on these limpid days of west coast Indian summer. As I sit with my second cup of coffee under the enormous white arch that frames our little dining room, the leaves shimmer in the luminous morning light, all shades of gold and orange and green. I miss the brazen red of a New York October, but in its place there is the somber, saturated Emily Carr blue-green hue of the evergreens, the base color in this landscape of my soul. All through the winter it will provide a serene backdrop for the intermittent snowfalls of the region.

It seems fitting that I write these words at the rustic old pine table my parents bought for their first home, fifty years ago, and that the living room holds the mahogany desk, and the bedroom, the 1970s Formica-topped dresser and mirror that my father built three decades ago. Fitting, because I feel in a visceral as well as metaphorical sense that I have come full circle. After four years in England and a thirteen-year stint in New York, I have finally returned, bringing Steve with me.

Having stepped over the threshold into our new life, my inner eye gazes in two directions as I look back on all that has happened since I wrote my journal on simple living, then ahead to what it will mean to continue my search for simplicity in this place I have reclaimed as home. What does it mean to live simply in the most expensive city in Canada, where even a humble bungalow in the desirable but not luxurious westside neighborhood where we now live and would like soon to buy, sells for half a million dollars? We will have to be very clear about what we need in terms of space and amenities, that much seems certain. We may even decide to move farther out, after all, if it turns out that space is our first priority.

Meanwhile we purchased our first car in fifteen years, a 2000 Toyota Camry in a pearly taupe poetically advertised as "antique sage." Although we'd planned to buy a good used one, we found that due to its popularity, the Camry commands a very high price, so we are happily enjoying the new-car-smell and the smooth ride. After debating whether we should replace our ancient fourteen-inch box at all, we also bought a new television set. And next spring I plan to leave the dark ages of computer technology by upgrading to one that can support the Internet. I can no longer deny the cumulative evidence that e-mail correspondence is the wave of the future. And perhaps, in ways I cannot quite imagine yet, that too can assist my attempt to live more simply.

*

My heart feels full so much of the time. Everything around me is resonant with memory that undergirds present experience with richness and depth, and I am often reminded of my uncertain younger self, full of passionate intensity and enormous hunger to be recognized and loved. In New York, I sometimes wondered if I'd be looking for ghosts when I finally returned to Vancouver, for a life that had ended forever with my move to England. When I wander through the student union building to the cafeteria to pick up cinnamon buns for brunch, visceral memories flood through me and I almost expect to see my eager twenty-two-year-old self two steps before me, scanning the room for a familiar face or an empty table at which to write. Twenty-five years ago I wondered how, out of all the people in the world, I would ever meet my soul mate. Now I'll take my cinnamon buns back to the apartment, put on a fresh pot of coffee, and eat a late breakfast with Steve.

Aware that my experience is subjective rather than absolute, I nevertheless feel more solid here, more substantial, at once safer and more visible, more embedded in my surroundings, no longer the "resident alien" my green card reminds me I am in New York. Here I feel part of the natural beauty that floods my senses and soul; somehow the frequency is right. Even though we have yet to begin the process of finding a permanent home, I am no longer provisional or temporary. I no longer feel that our lives are on hold.

As I'd expected, our coast-to-coast move afforded the best possible impetus to streamline, unclutter, and simplify. For six months, I sorted—passing on, donating, and throwing out the "stuff" of our lives, and finally packing what remained into bags, boxes, and cartons. A move like this can never be simple—especially when sabbatical, immigration, and customs issues are involved—but I was determined to see it through with as much care and thoughtfulness as possible. Looking back now, I'm glad I took the time to do it that way.

One New York friend took several carloads of small furniture, household goods, and clothing, including several skirts I sewed years ago. Other friends took pots and pans, cassettes and CDs, books and bedspreads, more clothes, and bags of food. At the College, I made each of my students choose a book from my shelves, which most, touchingly, saw as a gift, while a few participated only under duress. Throughout the last workshop series on Staten Island, I placed a box of books in the middle of the living room, free for the taking, and continued to refill it week after week. The College library happily accepted several boxes of German literature and even sent a receipt for income tax purposes. Fifteen large garbage bags filled with clothes and bedding went to Project Hospitality for distribution to the homeless on Staten Island. A week before our moving date we called up an acquaintance with a used furniture shop and offered him everything we no longer wanted free of charge, with the condition that he had to take it all. He happily obliged and gave us a well-used but sturdy wooden office chair for Steve's study in exchange. Our trusty old 1986 Camry was picked up by a Jewish charitable organization, and we received another tax write-off in the mail.

And then, finally, at the end of June, we moved. And the stress got worse. And then it got better. And here we are, in October, in Vancouver, British Columbia.

Our present accommodation is smaller than what we had on Staten Island. Housework is minimal and quickly done; it doesn't get any simpler than this. With both of us working at home, however, we will need additional space for the long run. I need a room of my own—instead of a desk and bookcase in the living room and a computer worktable in the bedroom, while I conduct most of my work at the dining room table, next to the coffee pot. Soon we will begin looking for a home.

*

Draped over the back of the blue couch at the far end of the living room are various lengths of jewel-toned fabrics—midnight blue, forest green, plum wine, and deep burgundy—and an array of beautiful burnished gold trims, creamy laces, sequins, satin ribbons, and brilliantly hued crystal and cloisonné beads. My gypsy skirts, so long deferred, are in full swing, and provide such pleasure in the doing that for the life of me, I can't remember why I stopped making and wearing them twenty years ago. Did my gypsy self really go underground for all those years?

There is great sensual delight in choosing and handling the fabrics and trims, and playing with color, texture, and shape. The variations to date include my "Indian" skirt (antique gold on black, with sequin trims in brilliant blue, purple, and green); a "Slavic" skirt (satin ribbons in rose and teal, floral lace, pearls from an old necklace, and embroidery); a "Persian" skirt (red and black braid twisted with gold); and, my latest, a "Spanish" skirt (wide bands of sparkling blue and purple sequin trims on black). My next design will be mauves and blues on a plum background.

As friends and strangers ask about the origins of my skirts, I have been prompted to think about the meaning of *gypsy* for me. When I was a little girl my mother referred to me as "Zigeunerin" because I wanted to travel and often seemed a misfit in my own family. "Did you steal me from the gypsies?" I asked. "Yes, we did," she said. "Is that what you want me to say?"

The Outsider, the one not welcome, the one outside the collective who refuses to abide by society's dictates, the perpetual wanderer with no permanent home, the wild one, free spirited and uncontainable. The archetypal resonance of gypsy has been so powerful for me, surfacing vividly in my dreams and now, once again, finding tangible expression in my beautiful skirts. My imagination, my creativity, my fantasy of all the exotic lives I might have led in other times and places—all are reflected in my darkly shimmering skirts.

They also carry the energy of my Shadow, the flamboyant and reckless underside of my serenely responsible, balanced Libra temperament, unashamedly lusty and passionately in love with color and music and dance. I've been dipping into Thomas Moore's *The Soul of Sex: Cultivating Life as an Act of Love.* He surely would say that my skirts are a manifestation of my desire to eroticize the world, to immerse myself in beauty and sensual delight. And he would be right.

This is a lot of meaning for my gypsy skirts to carry. But it's all there, in those richly-hued fabrics and exotic, luxurious trims. Other people respond to them as well, perhaps recognizing something familiar, as if they too respond to this archetypal energy. And no, my powerful affinity is not altered in the least by the knowledge that historically, gypsies have been as obsessed with purity as any fundamentalist religion, and harsh to the extreme with perceived violators to their rigid moral codes. Both *Latcho Drom*, Tony Gatlif's stunning documentary of Gypsy music and dance, and Isabel Fonseca's wonderful account, *Bury Me Standing: The Gypsies and Their Journey*, held me in thrall, as if the gypsies' story were also my own.

*

All summer and into the fall we have feasted on organic fruits and vegetables from my parents' garden. Every week we receive an abundance of produce, more than we can possibly eat. In New York we were thrilled to find kirby cucumbers and Jersey tomatoes at the greenmarket, the closest thing to fresh garden produce available on Staten Island, even though they were not organic. This summer the garden has yielded red and yellow potatoes, carrots, romaine and butter lettuce, tomatoes, cucumbers, green beans, yellow beans, beets, zucchini, kohlrabi, onions, broccoli, green and red cabbage, leeks, kale, Swiss chard, parsnips, Brussels sprouts, parsley, chives, dill, savory, oregano, and the first acorn squash of the season. Fruitwise, we have enjoyed raspberries, blackberries, gooseberries, plums, pears, peaches, apricots, grapes, and several varieties of apples. The harvest has provided hazelnuts and walnuts as well. What bounty!

Every year in recent times my mother has sworn off gardening because of her painful back and the endless work involved. Every spring my father prepares the soil and they begin anew.

Last weekend again, Mum said, "I told Dad that maybe next year we won't have a garden. For the little that we eat, all that work?" She looked at me to see my response, but I just smiled at her. She smiled back and said, "You've heard that before, haven't you?"

"Yes," I said, "and the year you really don't plant a garden, I'll worry."

"The year I really don't have a garden, I'll be dead," she responded.

"I know," I said. "That's what I mean. Just keep planting that garden."

The thrill of watching an empty expanse of rototilled and freshly fertilized earth almost perceptibly give rise to the copious lush green leafiness of a dozen kinds of vegetables is irresistible, it seems. The garden is extravagant, such luxuriant leafy splendor, at the heart of which—one beautiful, shimmering dark green head of broccoli.

*

Gradually I am picking up threads of my former life in Vancouver, aware that it will be a very different tapestry Steve and I weave over time in our shared life here. At the culmination of a productive thirty-year professorship in psychology and philosophy, he is happy to immerse himself in his writing all day and head out for a long walk with me before dinner. He is more mellow and content than I have ever seen him in our fifteen years together.

The temptation to make up for lost time beckons—I want to do everything and see everyone at once—but aware of how stressful the past year has been, we've done things slowly, preferring to spend quiet days working, then walk by the ocean at sunset, visit my parents, and explore our new-old surroundings. Gradually I am reconnecting with old friends from my former life here. Although our cherished Yamaha piano traveled far to join us on the west coast, mysteriously we have not made much music to date. Spring will no doubt awaken my musical energy anew and I will audition for the Vancouver Bach Choir once again. Then I'll discover what my rusty midlife vocal chords can do.

After planning to teach part-time in order to augment our sabbatical half-pay, I decided not to rejoin the ranks of the academically exploited and am content to teach only a six-week journal class for the university's Writing Center this fall. More than anything I look forward to starting up the Women's Journal Workshop West in the spring, with the hope that I can foster the same sense of vital and loving community that evolved in the Staten Island circle in our ten years together. A low-tech grassroots approach seems called for again. I know that if I continue the work to the best of my ability, those who are meant to will find their way to the workshop. At some deep level I believe that "if I build it, they will come."

As far as FI (Financial Independence) is concerned, it seems that we are in good shape. Barring a drastic turn in our fortunes, we should be pretty well set for our respective full-time writing endeavors. The fact that taxes are significantly higher across the board in Canada than in the U.S. is largely offset by the favorable U.S. to Canadian dollar exchange rate in recent years. I feel more relaxed about money in general now that we are actually here, but our "selective frugality" won't change much now, since that's what has allowed us such freedom at this point in our lives. In spite of the most expensive housing costs in Canada, Vancouver offers an excellent quality of life. With its temperate climate and access to ocean and mountains, its ethnic diversity and abundance of cultural life, most of what we need and want is readily accessible.

Now that we have achieved the life we worked so hard for, how will I use my time and life energy? Just past my forty-seventh birthday, I look ahead to an anticipated thirty or forty years of freedom. What will I do with the second half of my "wild and precious life"?

*

Six weeks before we moved, I participated in an eight-day BodySoul Rhythms Intensive Workshop with Jungian analyst Marion Woodman and her co-leaders, Mary Hamilton and Ann Skinner. I'd wanted to do it for several years, and although the timing seemed all wrong for practical purposes, a voice deep inside me insisted, "Do it. Now." Steve, too, felt it was important for me and so, despite our shared misgivings about the timing, I boarded the bus to Lenox, Massachusetts. Although it was anything but simple to orchestrate, this turned out to be the right thing to do and the right time to do it. The profound experiences and insights shared there with thirty-five other women have nurtured me ever since and continue to resonate, providing a tuning fork for the rest of my life.

After an early-term miscarriage in 1998, it now seems unlikely that my dear forty-seven-year-old body will bear a child. If that be the case, I am open to a grand new passion for the second half of my life, something that will demand the best of my creative energy and love. The BodySoul leaders, as it turns out, are creating a training program to expand the work they are doing, a program that will carry forward the orthodox curriculum of Jungian studies to include not only mind and spirit, but body and soul in the most immediate and concrete way. To my delight, this training will be offered in part on one of the Gulf Islands, just several short ferry rides away from Vancouver. Synchronicity indeed. For the past five years, I have worked mainly with Jungian themes in my own workshops, focusing on the writing of Jungian women such as Esther Harding, Helen Luke, Marion Woodman, and many others. This training may open the door to that grand passion I seek.

In a world starving for Mother, let my loving maternal energy not go to waste. Let my heart and soul open to the world, my sturdy arms and legs find work that will heal those I meet and, in the process, myself as well. Let my spoken and written words bless those around me with truthfulness, comfort, and delight, and let my voice grace them with music. Let my vulnerable heart release past resentments, forgive old wounds, and be replenished each morning with tenderness, humor, and loving-kindness.

I know this is a tall order. But I am going to do my damndest.

*

My orientation has reversed. The relative weights of my east coast and west coast lives have shifted. Three months to the day from our departure, I returned to New York as a visitor for the first time—and discovered, as I'd suspected, that when I don't have to live there, New York holds all the excitement and fascination for which it is fabled. From the vast sea of lights that greets the air traveler in descent to the adrenaline kick of its pulsating streets, Manhattan is charged with endless possibility; I am stimulated and overstimulated, ferociously energized in an "I can do anything" sort of way. There's so much to see and explore, to discover and enjoy. (My best afternoon was spent returning to the fabric district which I'd finally discovered just months before we left, feasting my eyes on the endless rows of fabric and trims, and stocking up for the additional gypsy skirts I'm planning. Brilliant hues of purple and magenta, blue and green, luscious reds and oranges, burnished golds and gleaming silvers; store after store overstocked with glorious ribbons and laces, glowing and catching the afternoon sunlight. What joy!)

But it is also *too much*. Overwhelmingly noisy. Massive. Aggressive. Dirty. Ruthless. Claustrophobic. I need more space, more air, more green, fewer skyscrapers and more sky. Apart from having to leave, again, my dear workshop community after our intensive fall workshop series, I was relieved to return to our slower, gentler, greener life in Vancouver. But it's clear now that I will embrace the Big Apple as an occasional visitor far more wholeheartedly than I was ever able to as a resident. Who can account for the vagaries of place-affinities? Who can explain our soul connections with what we call "home"?

*

In my Saturday morning journal class, I look out a huge picture window with a breathtaking view of the tree-covered mountains of West Vancouver sloping down to English Bay. From time to time a seagull floats by with curved grace; otherwise the vista is untroubled by motion. As my students write to the lyrical strains of "Secret Garden," sip coffee, and nibble on zucchini walnut muffins I baked for them last night, my gaze is held for an endless moment, and I am transfixed by the long-yearned-for beauty of it all. My soul is deeply at rest here, my heart, so thankful. My body is at home.

Marlene Schiwy
Vancouver, B. C.

Appendix:
Writing Suggestions
on Simple Living

Here are some of the questions I considered in my "journal of simple living." If you are trying to unclutter your life, you might want to explore them in your own journal.

- What matters most?
  How much is enough?
  What are the bare bones of my life?
  What is essential, and what superfluous?
  How do I want to spend my days?
  What is my life energy for?
  What does simple living mean to me?
  What are the areas in my life I'd most like to simplify?

- Rilke advised the young poet to "love the questions themselves" and to "live everything, live the questions now." What are the big questions in my life right now? What would it mean for me to live them—patiently and consciously?

- Where is there clutter in my life? How would my life be different if I sorted it out? What is preventing me from doing it?

- How would I describe my relationship with time? What is my time for? How much time do I need? How much time do I have? When do I feel myself flowing in time? When do I feel at war with time?

- How do I feel about money? What does money buy me? What does money not buy? How much money do I need? How will I earn it?

- How do I feel about my environment? Does the landscape around me nurture my soul? If not, why I am here? Does my home reflect my values and passions? Does it provide comfort and refuge from the demands of the world? If I could live wherever I want, where would I be? If not where I am right now, what would it take for me to get there?

- If I didn't have to work for a living, how would I spend my time?
  What creative projects would I immerse myself in, if time and energy and resources were plentiful?
  If I suddenly discovered I had only a year to live, what would I do with that year?

- What do I *need* in my life?
  What do I *want* in my life?
  What is it I *cannot live without?*

- If I had to summarize my life's purpose in three words or phrases, what would they be?

- What would it mean to simplify my relationships and the way I communicate with others? Are there relationships in my life that no longer serve a purpose, that need uncluttering in order to create time and space for something new?

Below are some writing topics that people found useful in my "Journal Writing and the Art of Simple Living" workshop series.

- Briefly outline a typical day in your life. Start with the ring of the alarm clock and briefly list (in point form) everything you do throughout the day right until you are in bed.

  Then go through and highlight or check off those activities that you find most meaningful and satisfying in the doing.

  Go through a second time, this time marking any activities that seem to have no redeeming value or meaning to your life, or those you do only under duress.

  Then ask yourself, how can I minimize the latter in order to create more space for the former, and perhaps explore new ventures and projects?

- Ask yourself three questions:
  How much do I really need?
  How much do I really want?
  How much am I willing to do to get what I want?

    If the answer to the third question is, "Much less than I'm doing now," you're ready to choose the simpler life.[49]

- Rapid Writing Exercises. Write for five or ten minutes on each of the following:
  Simplicity
  Time
  Clutter

  If I had more time, I would . . .
  If I had more freedom, I would . . .
  If I were more creative, I would . . .
  If I had more money, I would . . .

  Simple living means . . .
  The area of my life that most needs simplification is . . .
  If I could simplify this, I'd be able to . . .

  If I could, I would like to stop . . .
  If I could, I would love to begin . . .
  If I could, I would be happy to increase . . .

  What are the values I hold dearest?
  How do I embody them in my daily life?
  How can I live them more fully?

- How would you describe your life—in ten or twelve words, phrases, or metaphors? Which *one word* best sums it up? Write an expanded journal entry on that one.

- *"Rags to Riches"*

  Suppose you were suddenly reduced to dire poverty. What things in your possession or lifestyle would you struggle hardest to preserve? Expand on your feelings about these things in your writing.

  Suppose again that you fell heir to a fabulous fortune. What would you do first? Write about this. Then what?

  When you have finished, note any things which suggest themselves as possible changes in your lifestyle right now.[50]

- Here is an exercise about envisioning a truly fulfilling life.
  — What did you want to be when you grew up?
  — What have you always wanted to do that you haven't yet done?
  — What have you done in your life that you are really proud of?
  — If you knew you were going to die within a year, how would you spend that year?
  — What brings you the most fulfillment—and how is that related to money?
  — If you didn't have to work for a living, what would you do with your time?[51]

  After you have reflected on several of these questions in writing:

  What does your writing reveal about your true passions in life? Would someone just getting to know you be able to recognize them? If not, why are they suppressed or hidden away?

Finally, here is a guided visualization exercise for which you will want to allow plenty of time and which you may want to come back to more than once.

Mapping Your Life

Take two sheets of blank paper and draw on each the outline of a "continent" that represents your life. Draw any shape that feels true to your experience of your life; it might be a circle, a mandala, a geometric shape, or a random doodle. Let your hand move freely across the page.

On the first one, divide this shape into areas that represent how much time and energy are currently devoted to various parts of your life such as family obligations, work and professional life, homemaking, study, commuting, friendship, leisure, personal maintenance, etc. Do this intuitively, the way it seems to you—without too much deliberation. You can also use colors that express your feelings about each area. You may wish to subdivide each part further, for example, within homemaking, you might include shopping, cooking, and cleaning. Do this now, before you read on.

The second outline represents your ideal world. Apportion your time and energy accordingly. Keep in mind that some areas on the first map may disappear entirely and you may add new ones. Don't try to second-guess yourself; do it as spontaneously as possible. Map out your life to suit yourself, as you would choose to live it, if time and money were not considerations. Be extravagant.

Now take a careful look at your two life maps. Note where they overlap and where they diverge. When you have contemplated them, consider the following questions in your journal.

What is the most significant overlap between the two? What is the greatest difference between them? Are you surprised by what you have drawn?

What is your overall feeling about the first map? What associations do you have to the shape of your life as you drew it there? What areas occupy the most time and space? What colors did you use, and what do they represent?

212

How do you feel as you look at the second map? How is it different from the first one? What is the most striking thing about it? What is gone, and what new elements have you introduced into your ideal life? How have the proportions changed?

What would it take for you to create more harmony and overlap between the two? Are there new elements on the second map that you could bring into your life right now? In particular, can you find one new dimension to begin exploring right now?

Please note: Since many of us are crammed full of mental "shoulds" and "ought-tos," *mapping out* our lives before writing about them provides a way of allowing feelings and intuitions to be expressed beyond the control of the verbal censor. What emerges is often more expressive of our heart's truth than words alone. The map of your ideal life can also be expanded into a collage, with additional images, pictures, or anything else that represents the shape your ideal life would take.

Notes

1. Etty Hillesum, *An Interrupted Life: The Diaries, 1941-43*, p. 106.

2. Helen Nearing, *Loving and Leaving the Good Life*, p. 100.

3. Frank Levering and Wanda Urbanska, *Simple Living*, p. 8.

4. Joe Dominguez and Vicki Robin, *Your Money or Your Life*, p. 279.

5. Carol Orsborn, *Enough Is Enough*, p. 161.

6. Anne Morrow Lindbergh, *Gift from the Sea*, p. 103.

7. May Sarton, *The House by the Sea*, p. 28.

8. William Stafford, "A Ritual to Read to Each Other," cited in Marion Woodman, *Leaving My Father's House*, p. 351.

9. Mary Catherine Bateson, *Composing a Life*, p. 133.

10. Julia Cameron, *The Artist's Way*, p. 83.

11. Henry David Thoreau, *Walden*, pp. 52, 53.

12. Etty Hillesum, *An Interrupted Life*, p. 75.

13. Anne Morrow Lindbergh, *Gift from the Sea*, p. 28.

14. Steven M. Rosen, "Wholeness as the Body of Paradox," in *Journal of Mind and Behavior*, p. 422.

15. Etty Hillesum, *An Interrupted Life*, pp. 17, 18.

16. Helen Luke, "Inner Relationship and Community," in *The Way of Woman*, pp. 41, 42.

17. Christa Wolf, "Speaking of Büchner," in *The Author's Dimension*, p. 176.

18. May Sarton, *The House by the Sea*, pp. 59, 60.

19. Helen Luke, "A Freedom to Be Oneself," in *The Way of Woman*, p. 187.

20. Helen Luke, "The Sense of Humor," in *The Way of Woman*, p. 78.

21. Marion Woodman, *Conscious Femininity*, p. 101.

22. Anne Morrow Lindbergh, *Gift from the Sea*, p. 58.

23. Helen Nearing, *Loving and Leaving the Good Life*, pp. 104, 193, 194.

24. Marion Woodman, "The Body's Wisdom," in *On Women Turning Sixty*, pp. 112, 115.

25. Toni Morrison, "Chloe Wofford Talks About Toni Morrison," by Claudia Dreifus, *The New York Times Magazine*, September 11, 1994, p. 75.

26. Drew Leder, *The Absent Body*, pp. 80, 163.

27. Eva Hoffman, *Lost in Translation*, p. 274.

28. Sue Bender, *Plain and Simple*, pp. 6-8.

29. Elisabeth Kübler-Ross, *The Wheel of Life*, p. 286.

30. Natalie Goldberg, *Wild Mind*, p. 138.

31. Marion Woodman, *Conscious Femininity*, p. 48.

32. Stephen Nachmanovitch, *Free Play*, p. 148.

33. Carolyn G. Heilbrun, *The Last Gift of Time*, p. 128.

34. Etty Hillesum, *An Interrupted Life*, pp. 196, 203.

35. Helen Luke, "Suffering," in *The Way of Woman*, p. 57.

36. Alberto Melucci, *The Playing Self*, pp. 19-21.

37. Anne Morrow Lindbergh, *Gift from the Sea*, p. 115.

38. Wendell Berry, "The Wild Rose," cited in Anne Lamott, *Bird by Bird*, p. xxvii.

39. Drew Leder, *The Absent Body*, p. 163.

40. Helen Luke, "The Life of the Spirit in Women," in *The Way of Woman*, pp. 24, 25.

41. Nelle Morton, *The Journey Is Home*, p. 205.

42. Helen Luke, "Money and the Feminine Principle of Relatedness," in *The Way of Woman*, pp. 43, 47, 48.

43. Stephen Nachmanovitch, *Free Play*, pp. 163, 164.

44. Elisabeth Kübler-Ross, *The Wheel of Life*, pp. 285, 286.

45. Marion Milner, *Eternity's Sunrise*, p. 1.

46. Helen Nearing, *Loving and Leaving the Good Life*, p. 151.

47. May Sarton, *Journal of a Solitude*, p. 160.

48. May Sarton, *Journal of a Solitude*, p. 89.

49. From *The Vancouver Province*, January 2, 1996.

50. This exercise is taken from *Keeping Your Personal Journal* by George Simons (New York, Ballantine, 1978, p. 172), now sadly out of print.

51. From *Your Money or Your Life*, by Dominguez and Robin, p. 110.